Kamloops History: Fictions, Facts and Fragments

Kamloops History: Fictions, Facts and Fragments

Wayne Norton

Plateau Press
Vancouver, British Columbia

Plateau Press
3230 West 5th Avenue
Vancouver, BC
Canada V6K 1V4

For Information please visit: www.plateaupress.com

Library and Archives Canada Cataloguing in Publication

Norton, Wayne, 1948-
Kamloops history: fictions, facts and fragments / Wayne Norton.

Includes bibliographical references.
ISBN 978-0-9698842-6-2

1. Kamloops (B.C.)—History. I. Title.

FC3849.K3N67 2007 971.1'72 C2007-905397-1

Cover design by Hazel Mader
Production by Mader & Associates, Kamloops, BC
Printed in Canada by Hignell Book Printing

Books from Plateau Press are distributed by:
Sandhill Book Marketing
Unit #4 - 3308 Appaloosa Rd
Millcreek Industrial Park
Kelowna, BC V1V 2G9
Order phone 1-800-667-3848

Table of Contents

Author's Foreword

When considering how to sum up the contents of this little book, I initially thought it best simply to say they are no more than a reflection of my own interests in Kamloops history—popular culture, politics and Tranquille. As the book progressed through various conceptual and practical stages, I realised that those interests actually are not nearly as narrow as such a short list would suggest. The city and its surrounding countryside have enjoyed a varied and fascinating history—and I find myself interested in all of it. Some familiar pages of that history are revisited here. I do hope that at least a few readers will be motivated by what they find in *Fictions, Facts and Fragments* to search elsewhere for information on other lesser known topics as well as for details of the many major themes of Kamloops history.

Even in a volume as slim as this, there are many people who must be thanked for their contributions. Before mentioning all those people, I must first acknowledge my gratitude to Hazel Mader and Shawne MacKay of Mader & Assoc., who provided not only essential production expertise and advice, but also equally essential enthusiasm and encouragement at times when it was needed most. For each of the articles included here, their support and suggestions were indispensable.

Apart from cited written sources, each article has benefited from the generous contribution of time and effort by many people. Sheila Park and Shirley Rhodes helped to track down memorabilia and photographs from the Riis years. Winston Putnam provided the Gaglardi campaign button, while the Arrex record was part of a collection purchased by the author many years ago from the estate of Ian Clarke. The article on Tranquille is a look at a still unfinished story and draws upon the knowledge of the many people who helped with the research for *A Whole Little City by Itself* and of those who still occasionally get in touch with interesting details about "life at the san."

Two articles are revisions of earlier work long out of print. "First Impressions" is a second look at a theme first examined in *Kamloops: One Hundred Years of Community*, published in 1992. The "Children's May Festivals" revisits the topic of the firemen's May Days, the subject of an article initially included in *Reflections: Thompson Valley Histories* in 1994. To all those who helped with the original articles, I am—once again—grateful.

The article on Mary Spencer and Bill Miner is a product—at least in part—of my long-held fascination with the Edwardian era. Roger Touche at Heritage House Publishing and Peter Grauer of Kamloops kindly permitted the covers of their books on Bill Miner to be included, and Don Stewart of MacLeod's Books in Vancouver was particularly generous in making his collection of rare Mary Spencer photographs available for inclusion in this book. Thanks also to the Kamloops Museum and Archives, Colin Browne, Doug Mackey of North Bay, and Jim McGraw and Chuck Davis of the Vancouver Historical Society.

The two essentially visual pieces—"Postcards from the Past" and "Collectables and Ephemera"—are the result of the much-to-be-admired inclination of some people to collect things. Winston Putnam made available several unusual items and put me in touch with Joyce Klassen and Don Wilson who generously allowed access to their extensive collection of Kamloops memorabilia. The number of credit lines making reference to them is an indication of how important their contributions were to the creation of this book. The wonderful fruit crate labels came to us through the efforts of veteran California collector Pat Robertson, who directed us to Vernon collectors Lorna and Larry Kotz. Others who deserve thanks are Gerry Bond, John Dietrich, Roy Forbes and Rein Stamm. Items without credit lines were likely found somehow in the chaos of the author's study.

Of course, the collector *par excellence* is the local museum. Archivist Susan Cross at the Kamloops Museum and Archives provided essential advice about how I might search for obscure photographs and information. You just can't do history in this town without depending upon the KMA—well, I never have. Past and present staff and the former board of directors deserve recognition and applause for the collections they have drawn together for the benefit of those interested in local history.

It does strike me that a revival of interest in the local past would be a welcome development. Considering the size of the city and the variety and depth of its historical experience, recent publications on Kamloops history seem remarkably few, though there are topics both large and small that would reward either academic or popular treatment. It is now forty years since Mary Balf, Colonel Vicars and their volunteers published their historical work on the early settlement period in Kamloops. As time passes, a major assessment of the city and district in the twentieth century seems increasingly overdue.

There certainly is nothing major about this small compendium of fictions, facts and fragments. All that is offered here are snippets and glimpses. Those who helped to put this book together find that such details are intrinsically fascinating because of the insight they provide into the elusive panorama that is the local past. It is our hope and belief that many people share that fascination.

Mel Rothenburger in Kamloops, Tim Percival in Vancouver, and Colin Grier of Washington State University were kind enough to take time from their busy schedules to read the complete text and to offer constructive suggestions. Despite all assistance received, any flaws and faults contained in these pages are of course attributable to the author alone. Finally, I must acknowledge a debt of gratitude to my wife Val. Though certainly not a collector, her acceptance of my apparently compulsive pursuit of books, records and sheet music, postcards and the many side roads of history in general makes so much seem within reach.

Wayne Norton
Kamloops and Vancouver
2007

First Impressions: When the Travellers Come to Town

In British Columbia today, there are few communities that do not invite travellers to stay and share in the attractions held dear by local residents. Kamloops advertises extensively to secure its share of these travellers, and in recent years has been quite successful in presenting itself as an attractive British Columbia tourist destination. Between the arrival of the railway in 1885 and the celebration of the city's centennial in 1993, thousands of tourists and travellers visited Kamloops. How did they see us? What opinions did they form of the community and its surrounding terrain? Some fragmentary and impressionistic evidence exists to provide at least partial answers to these questions. It is instructive to listen to these voices from the past—the voices of people who were neither civic boosters nor self-serving detractors seeking to bolster the reputations of rival communities.

Before the First World War

Visitors to the village of Kamloops in the mid 1880s found a community completely absorbed in speculation about the possible effects the arrival of the railway could have upon the community. Morley Roberts, an English novelist who passed through in 1884 during his tour of North America, noted that conversation at the bar of his hotel focused almost entirely upon the railway. It was, he noted, "the all absorbing topic, some prophesying prosperity, and some universal ruin and desolation as its result." Morley commented wryly on "the street of which Kamloops" consisted.

He was not impressed by the Secwepmec dwellings he observed across the Thompson River or by the "steep, barren and treeless mountain" that stood behind them. Continuing his journey towards the coast, Roberts began to alter his assessment of the local landscape, admitting grudgingly that the scenery out towards Savona was "desolate but beautiful."

The difficulty in appreciating the scenery of the Thompson country was typical of British travellers of the nineteenth century. Accustomed to the green and verdant landscapes of the United Kingdom, these early tourists generally viewed the climate and vegetation of the local region as unappealing. Those who found publishers for their travel memoirs rarely included more than a brief comment on the Kamloops region, but more often than not that comment referred to the arid nature of the climate and scenery.

With the Canadian West so distinctly a highlight of the international travel circuit after the completion of the Canadian Pacific Railway (CPR), it seems curious that so few travellers wrote about Kamloops. In pre-war photographic collections, too, the Kamloops region seems to have attracted little interest, with most professional and amateur photographers concentrating their attention almost exclusively upon the Rockies and the Fraser Canyon. Interestingly, this parallels the treatment the Thompson region received in CPR promotional literature, which was enthusiastic about the Rockies and the Fraser Canyon, but barely mentioned Kamloops at all.

Two factors combined to work against Kamloops receiving greater attention. In the eyes of tourists, the area suffered by comparison with the more spectacular and more obvious beauty of the Rocky Mountains, the Cascades, the Fraser Canyon, and coastal British Columbia. It is ironic that while most travellers claim to have been left speechless by the natural beauty they saw in these areas, they nevertheless filled volumes in attempting to describe them. But of Kamloops, they wrote little or nothing.

In fairness to the tourists, the photographers and the CPR, the transcontinental rail service itself is probably the main reason why Kamloops is largely absent from the travel literature, photographic collections and promotional advertising of the day. Heading west, the daily CPR passenger train arrived at Kamloops at 11:00 p.m., and left for Vancouver at 11:15; heading east, the train arrived at 2:55 a.m., and departed ten minutes later. Travellers en route literally saw nothing of the Kamloops region. They could not comment—favourably or otherwise—upon a district that was little more than a whistle-stop in the night.

And what of those who actually got off their trains here? In the early 1890s, they would have found a community with a population of approximately five hundred people, proud of the incorporation of their community as a city in 1893, and engaging energetically in the overstated boosterism so typical of settlements in western Canada at that time. The Kamloops-based *Inland Sentinel* newspaper frequently expressed the manner in which local citizens wanted their community to be seen.

Rail replaced river as the principal means of travel for visitors.
Courtesy of Joyce Klassen and Don Wilson

> *Calmly seated among encircling hills on the left bank of the Thompson River, Kamloops, like the ancient Jewish capital, is "beautiful for situation," and in the matter of climate, scenery, and all that goes to make a city desirable, it may truly also be called "the joy of the whole earth."*

This was not an opinion with which tourist Douglas Sladen would have agreed. Sladen, known to be writing a book about his travels in Canada, was accorded special treatment by the CPR. He was met at Kamloops by the superintendent of the railway's Pacific Division with a private railcar that was to be hitched to a scheduled freight train for a leisurely, daylight trip to the coast. He checked into the city's "principal hotel" (probably the Grand Pacific) at midnight to find the establishment decked out in black crepe. The hotel apparently had been the scene of an evening funeral, and Sladen observed that the Irish maids were still in tears. He soon learned to his further discomfort that his room was used once a week by a travelling dentist and smelled of disinfectant. He described the service as poor, and after a "miserable breakfast" at the hotel, left in a bad mood and reached for his pen. Anyone who has travelled can appreciate how unpleasant experiences with food and accommodation sour perceptions of the place being visited. Predictably, Sladen's memoir was not kind to Kamloops.

More significant than the impressions garnered from a stay of a few hours are the opinions resulting from an extended visit. Stanton Hope, a young Englishman off to see the world, arrived in Kamloops in April 1907 seeking temporary employment, which he found first with the Post Office and then with the Arrow Lakes Lumber Company. He admired the dependable Kamloops sunshine and was amused by the continuing effort to overstate the virtues of the city. The population of Kamloops, he wrote, "was 2500, 3000, and 5000, according respectively to the census officers, the local inhabitants and the real estate agents." Hope wryly described Kamloops as "a pleasant little spot... as law-abiding as the rest of B.C.," and though he did not intend to settle, he entered for a quarter-section from the Dominion Lands Branch before leaving for Vancouver in September. His published recollections fondly describe Kamloops as a colourful mix of loggers, miners and cowpunchers, Europeans, Chinese, East Asians and Shuswap.

More famous, though of about the same duration, was the stay of Robert Service from July to November 1904. Like Stanton Hope, Service commented on the sharp social distinctions among the professionals, the trades people and the working men. He also suggested that his employer, the Bank of Commerce, was suspected of transferring its consumptive employees to Kamloops, where they might benefit from the invigorating air. Not consumptive himself, Service took up polo but seemed to enjoy most his rides in the surrounding hills. Yet, he, too, saw those hills with an unappreciative eye.

> *Life was pleasant, and the work was light. At four o'clock we were on our horses, riding over the rolling ridges, or into spectral gulches that rose to ghostlier mountains. It was like the scenery of Mexico, weirdly desolate and aridly morose. A discouraged land, forbidding in its weariness and resigned to ruin.*

Still, Service regretted his transfer to Whitehorse and was sorry to leave what he described as his "delightful" life in Kamloops.

Just before the First World War, the city began to develop a sense of permanence and to attract favourable comment from visitors. The population increased five-fold between 1885 and 1905, and by the outbreak of the war stood at just under four thousand. George Fallis, the local Methodist minister at that time, described Kamloops as "a tidy little city," proud of its green boulevards and prepared to pay the price of constant watering in order to counter the effects of the Thompson Okanagan sun. Reverend Fallis wrote that some days were "as hot as the Sahara." It is noteworthy that he described the community in terms of the railway, and not fundamentally as a ranching centre. "Kamloops was a railway city. Small railway cities are noted for their family spirit and Kamloops was no exception."

An early automobile attracts attention in front of the Leland Hotel.
Courtesy of Joyce Klassen and Don Wilson

The emerging sense of community seems to have been severely strained, however, by the arrival of the Canadian Northern work crews. Fallis found his ministerial skills tested by the questionable honesty of some of the migrant workers, and another visitor to the city in 1913, Harold McCracken, thought everything he encountered about Kamloops was mixed up due to the construction work, which had drawn "the roughest of all elements of humanity, the riffraff and the unholy." Though the city welcomed the economic benefits, the increase in the "roughneck" population and the heavy traffic certainly caused problems. As McCracken noted, the muddy main street was being made muddier and cut deeper by big, slow-moving horse-drawn freight wagons loaded heavily with supplies.

Between the Wars

Though little commentary on the Kamloops region was created by travellers before the First World War, the years following the war produced even less. This is unfortunate because, by the 1920s, the small city of Kamloops had developed an established appearance and a feeling of coherence. It was something of a golden age—the city's first. However, the interests of travel writers had shifted away from the Canadian West to more exotic locations, and newspapers of the day—though they continued unashamedly to boost their communities—rarely employed their columns to consider how outsiders viewed it. Famous people certainly did come to Kamloops in the 1920s, most notably Winston Churchill and the Prince of Wales, but neither left a written record of his impressions.

One visitor of the 1920s, a missionary with the Church of England, was struck by the views presented during her three-mile descent into the city from Knutsford. She noted the lack of vegetation on the surrounding hills, but found them beautiful nevertheless, and was surprised by the green appearance of the city. With gardens and boulevards and trees established, Kamloops was beginning to develop its reputation as "the oasis in the desert," a reputation that was enhanced as the maturing gardens at Tranquille became one of the essential local sights for tourists.

The most notable travellers to the Kamloops region in the 1930s were not tourists, and none of them could afford to stay at the new Plaza Hotel or at any of the less expensive hotels and boarding houses. As a transportation centre and as the largest community between Calgary and New Westminster, Kamloops was a natural stop for the unemployed in their nomadic search for work during the 1930s. Two "hobo jungles" developed early in the decade. One, at the north end of the Red Bridge, was for BC transients only; the other, at Mission Flats, was for those who came from out-of-province. At the peak of the Depression, the two camps were said to hold a thousand people between them—this at a time when the population of Kamloops, according to the census of 1931, was just over six thousand.

Like the travellers who had preceded them, few of the transients recorded their impressions for posterity. However, the reputation of Kamloops amongst this group of travellers was distinctly favourable. Local merchants seldom gave full value for relief tickets, but the transients experienced the same short-changing elsewhere and, according to one surviving memoir, accepted it as "part of living in those days." Though theft was frequently resorted to elsewhere, the word apparently circulating in the hobo jungles was that Kamloops businesses and residences were not to be victimized. The transients consciously attempted to avoid contributing to an antagonistic relationship with a community that acted as if it understood their plight. The policies of the local police force under Chief Charles Anderson had much to do with this relationship, as this song lyric by one veteran of the hobo jungles indicates:

Oh, Kamloops is an A-l town
To tramps and hoboes, so crooks beware
For if you touch a thing not yours
Chief Anderson will be in your hair.
Where the River Thompson flows
The tramps and hoboes comes and goes,
Wherever they may meet you
With the B.S. they will greet you
Where the River Thompson flows.

Four decades later, in the dedication to his memoir, Sydney Hutcheson, another "guest" in the hobo jungle by the Red Bridge, indicated just how profoundly the impression of fairness remained with him even decades later. He wrote: "On behalf of all the unemployed of 1932, I would like to thank the citizens of Kamloops who are still around, for their patience and good fellowship...."

It was an impression confirmed in June 1935 by the single largest group of "tourists" the city had ever seen. The previous March, in an abandoned store building at the foot of Victoria Street, delegates from the federal relief camps in British Columbia decided to call a strike in an attempt to force Ottawa into a policy of "work and wages." From Kamloops the call went out and relief camp workers from all over the province converged upon Vancouver in support of the strike. Prime Minister R.B. Bennett refused to consider their demands. Frustrated by the government's prolonged silence, the strikers finally decided to take their message to Ottawa in person. Nearly one thousand men hopped on the CPR freight train leaving Vancouver on the evening of the third of June. Their first stop would be Kamloops.

One of the organizers later admitted that the morale of the strikers reached its lowest ebb when the train pulled into Kamloops the next afternoon. The expected welcoming committee, expressions of support and donations of much needed food were not there to greet them. Demoralized by the poor reception in Kamloops and by the lack of results after two months of protest meetings in Vancouver, the strikers seriously considered abandoning the On-To-Ottawa Trek.

They were greatly encouraged, however, by the community's response to the meeting they held in Riverside Park that evening. As trekker Ronald Liversedge later wrote: "The people of Kamloops might have been a little slow to move, but when they realized what was happening, their response was big and generous. All of Kamloops turned out to the meeting." A small collection of money was made, and the next morning, some local residents provided a hot breakfast and coffee. Many well-wishers were on hand to bid farewell to the trekkers, who were in a cheerful and optimistic mood as they left on the late afternoon east-bound freight. Clearly, genuine hospitality enhances a community's reputation and is long remembered.

Since 1945

The two decades following the Second World War brought steady prosperity and a change in the image of the city. Today, many local residents recall that period as the city's second "golden age." Residents were proud of statistics released in 1945 indicating that, on a per capita basis, the community had the highest incomes in the province, as well as the greatest numbers of telephones and refrigerators. An air of contentment prevailed, and visitors started to attribute to Kamloops a quality rarely mentioned before the war—a degree of charm.

Bruce Hutchison, probably the most respected and well-known Canadian journalist of the middle decades of the last century, paid a summertime visit to Kamloops in the late 1940s. From a location very near the current site of the war memorial, he looked down upon what he described as a "perfect river community"—10,000 people living "the ideal small-town life" amidst a forest of shade trees and profuse gardens. But Hutchison provided more than just another echo of the by then conventional theme of seeing Kamloops as an oasis in the desert. From his vantage point

The city's finest tourist accommodation for decades was the Plaza Hotel.
Courtesy of Joyce Klassen and Don Wilson

in Sa-Hali—then devoid of all residential and commercial development—he expressed a profound admiration for what he saw:

> *[You] can look down directly on the roof of the town and realize at once what skill and imagination went into its construction. All around it, to the edge of the last back yard, is parched and bare, but within the circle of the town lies a green island of trees and gardens..., while two lavish valleys give the inhabitant, at every turn, a new glimpse of distant beauty.*

He recognised that the Thompson River was the essential economic and social fact of life in Kamloops, and was pleased that, despite the efforts of the local Chamber of Commerce to promote an image of "what is known in America as progress," many people on the street were representative of a genuine western heritage and were not just "the denizens of bogus dude ranches."

These comments continued to be echoed by subsequent travellers for two decades. One visitor in the early 1960s wrote that Kamloops had a character unlike any other town in the west:

> *Tidy streets and modern shops in an island of trees and gardens, an eight-inch [annual] rainfall and sunshine on most days throughout the year are among its attractive features. Across the river in North Kamloops were many small fruit growers, a few of whom made more than a bare living; a friendly people, happy and contented with their way of life.*

Another visitor during this period, Vera Kelsey, observed that women in Kamloops "were smarter in dress, grooming and posture" than elsewhere in the province. She noted that ranching as a way of life seemed to be in decline, but that Kamloops remained essentially "a cattle town." The maid at her hotel advised her that she had "come too late for our Rodeo and too soon for the Fat Cattle Show—the best things in town." When she asked why the pioneer brick and frame buildings were not well main-

Local dignitaries greet Prime Minister Mackenzie King in 1940 and Princess Margaret in 1958. Kamloops Museum and Archives photograph numbers 3860 and 8276

Mail from Kamloops drew attention to local attractions.

tained, one city politician told her that Kamloops citizens "refuse to go into debt for the sake of appearances." He added, "We may be short on beauty and culture, but we sure are long on making dollars."

By the mid 1960s, however, as commercial and residential growth mushroomed, the favourable comments by tourists diminished. The change was both swift and dramatic. The same traveller who had found the city so contented and attractive in the early 1960s returned in 1966 and was not impressed by the high-rise office and residential additions to the older parts of town. Nor did he find appealing the new homes that "spread untidily into the hills and through the valleys." His most severe criticism, however, concerned the change in air quality:

> *Most alarming of the many changes was in the atmosphere, the wonderfully clean, clear air with high light intensity we remembered having given way to a prevailing haze of pulp smoke mixed with chemicals from an oil refinery, dependent on the vagaries of wind and other atmospheric conditions for its dispersal.*

Though Phil Gaglardi's famous comment about "the smell of money" muted local criticism of the new industries, poor air quality became one of the things which visitors began to comment upon about their stay in Kamloops.

The sports fishermen, too, had complaints to make about the changes development brought to the area. Steve Raymond, who visited the city regularly, thought that by the early 1970s Kamloops had "lost much of its charm" due to tremendous population growth. The fishing lakes were much more accessible by road, but those very roads were diminishing the fish stocks. Raymond was blunt in his assessment:

> *The engineers who design these things seem to exhibit a singular lack of understanding of their effects on the surrounding environment. Filling a stream with crushed rock, or building a highway along its length can destroy the fishery as surely as an overdose of cyanide.*

Still, with no general closed season on fishing, the Thompson region continued to be described by *Beautiful British Columbia* magazine as a "recreational paradise" of trails, hills and lakes.

The city began to struggle to impress visitors. With the decline of rail travel, it was the automobile that brought most tourists to the city primarily along the Trans-Canada and the Yellowhead routes. Many travellers gained their first impressions of Kamloops from the extensive strip developments along the East Trans-Canada Highway, were surprised by smell of the air, and often simply drove on. The naming of the annual fair as Spoolmak Days and events such

For over a half a century, Kamloops motels have offered accommodation to weary motorists.
Courtesy of Joyce Klassen and Don Wilson

as the banana-heaving contest were well intentioned attempts to promote tourism, but they contributed questionably to the image of a city that, by the mid 1970s, seemed to lack a clear and positive definition.

By the end of the century, more positive perceptions—comparable to those of the post-war years—were once again dominant. The centennial of 1993 had much to do with this change of perception. In celebrating one hundred years as a city, Kamloops drew attention to the achievements of its past, to the positive aspects of its present, and to the potential of its future. Decades of growth had produced a community large enough to offer a wide variety of services and amenities. Significant efforts had minimised the problem of air quality. Some of the features discovered by appreciative tourists in the 1990s were not new at all. The accessible compact downtown core and the romantic aura of the surrounding hills and valleys, for example, have long been acknowledged and admired by Kamloops residents.

It is ironic that, once again, affluent tourists are passing through Kamloops on railway excursions to and from the Rocky Mountains. Like the tourists of a century ago, their perceptions (and the perceptions of those who arrive by road or air) are to some extent within and, to some extent, beyond our control and influence. There will always be those who fail to see and appreciate the natural beauty in the arid surroundings of the Thompson country. The new generation of railway tourists, the skiers, the tournament visitors, the sports fishermen and others will all return to their home communities with impressions of their stay here. They will talk; they may write; they may record and make public their thoughts on the Internet. The people of Kamloops are certainly listening.

July 2&3-1956

COMMODORE CAFE

Where Everybody Meets and Everybody Eats

Good Morning!

Breakfast Menu

FRUITS AND JUICES

Orange Juice	.15	Stewed Prunes	.15
Fresh Orange Juice	.25	Apple Sauce	.15
Grapefruit Juice	.10	Stewed Figs	.20
Pineapple Juice	.10	Sliced Bananas and Cream	.35
Apple Juice Sun Rype Apples	.10	Sliced Oranges and Cream	.35
Tomato Juice	.10	Sliced Pineapple	.40
Half Grapefruit	.15	Canned Pears	.35
Whole Grapefruit	.25	Peaches	.35

CEREALS

Choice of Cereals: Corn Flakes, All Bran, All Wheat, Puffed Wheat Grape Nuts, Grapenut Flakes, Bran Flakes, Puffed Rice, Shredded Wheat with Cream .15

Oatmeal with Cream	.15	Dry or Buttered Toast	.10
Cream of Wheat with Cream	.20	Dry or Buttered Toast with Jam, Marmalade or Honey	.15
Milk Toast	.20		
Cream Toast	.25	French Toast	.40
Hot Cakes and Syrup	.30	Buchwheat Cakes and Syrup	.35
Cinnamon Toast	.15		

Hot Cakes or Buckwheat Cakes with Ham, Bacon or Sausages or Two Eggs .20 extra

Tea, Coffee or Milk, 10c extra

BEVERAGES

Coffee	.10	Chocolate	.10
Pot of Tea	.10	Buttermilk	.10
Milk, glass	.10	Half and Half	.15
Ovaltine	.10	Oxo	.10

EGGS AND CHOPS

Only New Laid Eggs Served

Two Eggs, any style	.45	One Pork Chop, Two Fried Eggs	.85
Three Eggs, any style	.50		
Bacon ad Eggs	.80	One Lamb Chop, Two Fried Eggs	.85
Ham and Eggs	.80		
Fried Pork Sausages, Two Eggs	.80	One Veal Chop , Two Fried Eggs	.85
Fresh Hamburger Steak, Two Eggs	.85	Genuine Calves Liver, Two Fried Eggs	.80
Fried Tomatoes and Bacon or Ham	.80	Fried Swift's Ham or Bacon	.80

Bread and Butter included, Tea, Coffee or Milk.

A good breakfast at a good price is a traveller's necessity.

Courtesy of Joyce Klassen and Don Wilson

Postcards from the Past

The pace of modern life leaves little time for reflection. Ironically, all our labour-saving devices have combined only to enable us to labour longer. Looking forward is the prime focus of modern societies, as we work in hopes of achieving a better and more affluent future. Looking backwards requires a conscious, almost unnatural effort—an expenditure of time and energy that, for most, seems out of place in the rush to secure profit or in the attempt simply to survive.

Knowledge of the past can remind us that our daily routines and activities are part of a historical continuum. Without that knowledge, we simply do not know what remains the same and what has changed. It is common to speculate about how, if residents of fifty or a hundred years ago could have seen the future, they would have marvelled at the technological advances achieved by the generations that followed them. Of course, like us, they did not have the luxury of seeing into the future. No technological wonder has yet granted the human race that ability. But we do all possess the ability to look backwards.

One of the easiest ways of looking into the past is through an examination of old postcards. As repositories of local history, postcards are at least as informative about their topics as the newspapers of the day, and, because they are both compact and visual, postcards provide very specific "snapshots" of time and place. They were used by residents or visitors to the community as a cheap and convenient way of sending brief messages to friends and relatives all over the world. The postcards shown here conveyed images—and often, as an added bonus on their reverse sides, the senders' written impressions—of the small city located at the confluence of the North and South Thompson rivers.

It is tempting to say that these postcards show Kamloops as it was, but it must be admitted that in some cases they show Kamloops as it never was. In a very real sense, however, they have been sent from the past to the present to remind us, if not actually of where we have been and who we really once were, at least of how we perceived ourselves and how we were once perceived. Looking at them closely provides us with an opportunity to think about the past, the present and the future.

The faces of professional Edwardian models convey a suggestion of style and sophistication.

Scenes from early Kamloops. The bottom image remains the city's most famous postcard.
Courtesy of Joyce Klassen and Don Wilson

SEYMOUR STREET AND POST OFFICE, KAMLOOPS, B.C.

Above and Opposite: Four street scenes convey a sense of the city in the first half of the twentieth century. Courtesy of Joyce Klassen and Don Wilson

Seymour St., Kamloops, B. C.

LOOKING SOUTH ON FOURTH AVENUE KAMLOOPS. B C

The Old Men's Home and the Courthouse represented the city's finest architecture before the First World War.

People could relax at Bridal Falls on Peterson Creek or welcome a prime minister to town.
Courtesy of Joyce Klassen and Don Wilson

Above and Opposite: Four water scenes from a century ago reveal a very small settlement community where the rivers meet. Courtesy of Joyce Klassen and Don Wilson

Thomson River and Bridge at Kamloops, B.C.
105,808.

KAMLOOP SAW MILL.

Panoramic views often show Mount Peter and Mount Paul.

Commerce, residences and recreation all clung to the river.
Courtesy of Joyce Klassen and Don Wilson

Above and Opposite: Four views of Victoria Street show the transition from horses to automobiles and the introduction of traffic lights.

Courtesy of Joyce Klassen and Don Wilson

Kamloops in the 1920s under odd psychedelic skies.

Eight real photographs and one surreal representation of Kamloops.

Kamloops, B.C.

Postcards from the 1960s and 1970s rarely matched the artistry of those from earlier decades.

The Children's May Festivals

Like most communities in the Canadian West at the dawn of the twentieth century, Kamloops was much concerned with enhancing its image as a dynamic and progressive place to live. Rivalries with Vernon and Revelstoke were already well developed, but it was the rapid development of the coastal cities of New Westminster and Vancouver that Kamloops most sought to emulate. At the same time, the small middle class here shared in the emerging national consensus that the education and nurture of children were responsibilities to be shared by parents and the community. These circumstances and ambitions combined to produce the May Festivals—one of the most enduring traditions in this city's history.

The first community in British Columbia to establish a May festival was New Westminster, where the local fire department first organised the event as early as 1870. Members of the Kamloops Fire Department, eager to prove that the Kamloops brigade was the equal of that in any coastal city, made plans in the spring of 1903 for what they called the "Firemen's May Day." Their intention was to create an event that the children of the city could look upon as their very own. Activities were planned for the first day of May to include a programme of sports, dances and ceremonies that would appeal to a generation of children fascinated by tales of fairies, pixies, pirates and Robin Hood. Expenses would be covered by charging a nominal entrance fee to those wanting to observe the activities. The high point of the day would be the crowning of the young girl selected by the children themselves as their "Queen of the May."

The organisers made it clear that the events were to be open to all children regardless of school affiliation, but were disappointed when the Sisters of St. Ann, perhaps uncomfortable with the pre-Christian origins of May festivals, decided their students would not take part. The public school, however, embraced the idea with enthusiasm, and trustees declared Friday, May 1st to be an official school holiday. In mid April by secret ballot, the children elected thirteen-year-old Edith Lee as their first May Queen. She in turn selected her maids of honour: Trixy Vicars, Irene McCrum, "Tottie" Irwin and Annie Philips. Pearl Campbell, for ceremonial purposes, was chosen to play the role of "ex-queen." The business community endorsed the firemen's proposal and asked the mayor to proclaim a full public holiday. He did so, and all was ready for the city's first May Day.

The sports events began at 10 a.m. at Alexandra Park near the north end of the White Bridge. At the same time, parade participants began to gather downtown at the Kamloops Musical and Athletic Association Hall in preparation for the procession down Main Street and across the bridge to the park. Rather later than planned, the parade finally set off just after one o'clock. It included the sixteen-piece Rocky Mountain Rangers band (in its first public appearance), a guard of honour from the boys' brigade, uniformed firemen, a special carriage for the mayor and his aldermen, and numerous other carriages and pedestrians. A separate carriage was reserved for Pearl Campbell, Edith Lee and her maids of honour, all of whom, according to the *Inland Sentinel*, "looked dainty and sweet and made a pretty picture."

Amidst speeches and applause and the strains of "God Save The Queen," Edith Lee was crowned. Her first words as monarch commanded the festivities to continue. The Maypole dance was performed, and the dancers each received a piece of the ribbon as a souvenir of Kamloops' first May Day. All children in attendance were given candies and oranges, and the sports events were resumed. The parade was then re-formed to accompany the royal party to Queen Edith's home, where her mother provided dinner for her royal and civic guests. At 8 p.m., the dance at the Association Hall began, with adults permitted on the floor before 10 o'clock only if their dance partners were children. By the time the last waltz ended at 2 a.m., the firemen and school and city officials were assured that the day had been an unqualified success.

Following this pattern, the firemen organised successful May Days for nearly a decade. In 1904, it was decided to begin the sports events after the crowning of the new queen. From 1905 onwards, unless the designated day fell on a Saturday, city council declared only a half-holiday, rather than a full day. Beginning in 1907, the festivities were held in the grove near the new Red Bridge because the Alexandra Park grounds were thought to be "too dry and dusty for comfort." At some point, too, after the first few years, participation of boys was restricted to the sports events as the maypole dances and ceremonies were reserved strictly for the girls.

Each year, the carriage conveying the royal party to the park was decorated with bunting and colourful ribbon, while other decorated carriages and bicycles became more numerous with each successive May Day. The home of the queen was usually decorated both inside and out, often including garlands of flowers and ribbons on or around the dinner table. For the queen, her maids of honour, and the female maypole dancers, the most enchanting decorations were the dresses made especially for them by their mothers from the finest and most expensive fabrics. Clearly, the families honoured by the selection of their daughters donated significant amounts of both time and money to sustain the magic of the day. Just as clearly, less affluent families could not allow their daughters to entertain royal aspirations. The costs involved in dressmaking and in providing the May Day banquet for as many as eighteen people were substantial.

The designation of queen brought both privilege and civic responsibility. Queen Mary Barnhart, for example, laid the cornerstone of the new fire hall in 1905 using an elegant silver trowel provided by the mayor and inscribed with the date, description of the occasion and her name. Buried in a time capsule beneath the cornerstone were copies of *The Sentinel* and *The Standard*, and photographs of the mayor, his aldermen, and the firemen. Queen Mary was presented with the silver trowel as a keepsake. For a few years before the Great War, the queens acted as representatives of the city by sending telegrams of congratulation to their counterparts in New Westminster. In 1913, Kamloops May Queen Olive McLean wired to her counterpart in New Westminster "cordial greetings and sincere wishes for a bright and joyous reign over a happy people in a prosperous realm." She received in reply a telegram phrased in the required regal style:

> *On the occasion of your accession to the throne of Kamloops we, Jean McPhail, today crowned Queen of Westminster, extend cordial greetings [and] express our heartiest wishes for a successful and prosperous era in your kingdom during your rule. May your youthful subjects be as loyal and true to Your Majesty as our subjects here promise to be. May Peace and Prosperity attend all the days of our reign.*

Throughout the pre-war years, the May festivals were covered by both local newspapers as front page news. The queens and their entourages were invariably described as charming, pleasing, picturesque, sweet or dainty. As early as 1907, just four years after it had begun, the newspapers began to refer to the event as a "time-honoured" Kamloops tradition. Estimates of the numbers of children involved, of carriages and decorated motor cars in the procession and of spectators were used to gauge the success of the day's activities. Astonishingly, as many as one thousand children were said to have taken part in 1912 and again in 1913; more

The royal parties of 1910 and 1913.

Kamloops Museum and Archives photograph numbers 530 and 351

believable are the claims that thirty automobiles were counted in addition to horse-drawn rigs in the May Day parades during the years just before the First World War. The firemen received annual accolades from the newspapers for their efforts. *The Standard* in particular took great delight in reporting on the "Fire Laddies' Annual Day."

May Day was not without its critics and controversies. Expressing concern about the loss of instructional time and the emotional strain upon the candidates for queen, the school trustees voted to deny the school holiday in 1908. However, pupils and teachers united with the organisers in ignoring the trustees' wishes, and the festivities went ahead as planned. Two of the three school trustees resigned in protest, only to see their resignations applauded by the local press. Evidently, public opinion was strongly in favour of the continuation of the annual event.

Despite public support and acclaim, the firemen eventually were forced to admit that the festival had expanded to require more time and energy than were available within the fire department alone. In 1913, a committee of interested individuals took over responsibility for the Kamloops May Day. The committee made no changes to the structures it inherited from the firemen, but did begin the tradition of making public an annual statement of receipts and expenditures. The initial statement revealed that ticket sales had been very nearly sufficient to cover expenses, which had included the purchase of candies, oranges, ribbon, and flowers, the hire of rigs, bands and hall rental, and prize money for the sports events. When other donations were included, the committee was pleased to be able to bequeath $98.46 to the organisers of the 1914 May Day festivities.

The May festival of 1915 was remarkable in that, with only one exception, the queens of the previous thirteen years were all present. Their continuing residence in Kamloops suggests that the city, in the early years of the century, enjoyed a notable degree of social stability. It is also worth noting that, viewed collectively, the dozen former May Queens represented many of the families who formed the city's pre-war establishment. At least seven came from well known business or ranching families; six were daughters of mayors or aldermen.

Despite the outbreak of hostilities in Europe, the Kamloops May festivals were continued throughout the war years. Certain aspects of the event—most notably the parade—were reduced from the grandeur of the pre-war years, but the crowning ceremonies and the sports events still commanded the attention of children and adults alike. The city council granted full holidays for the first three festivals during the war, returning to the half holiday only in 1918. The event continued to find a space on the front pages of the newspapers, though the reportage was often linked to the war in Europe. The festival of 1915 raised $62 "for the installation of a bed in an English hospital for Canadian soldiers wounded at the front." One newspaper report linked the May Day to the war effort, insisting that men "begrimmed with the ravages of war, fighting on the battlefront or suffering from wounds in the hospital, will rejoice in the fact that the kiddies of Kamloops enjoyed the day."

The address of the May Queen to her loyal subjects, which followed a set pattern modified only slightly to suit the circumstances of the year in question, was customarily delivered not by the Queen but by the appointed Master of Ceremonies. The preparation of the speech certainly occurred under watchful adult eyes. During the war, the addresses underwent some predictable changes and urged the youth of the community to embrace an enhanced patriotism and willingness for sacrifice. Queen Reta McLean's address of 1918, like the speeches of the civic leaders and military men with whom she shared the podium, referred to Kamloops men fighting in Europe and to citizens at home working to support them. She concluded by advising all to invest wisely and to work for victory. Nevertheless, she signed

The royal parties of 1920 and 1921 are surrounded by patriotic symbols, serious citizens, and even more serious civic politicians.

Courtesy of Joyce Klassen and Don Wilson

her proclamation urging these virtues upon her subjects in traditional May Day fashion: "Reta, May Queen by virtue of election of the Dominion of Kamloops, North Kamloops, Powers Addition and the territories adjacent thereunto. Ruler of Entertainments and Empress of Hearts."

The decade following the war saw the May festivals achieve their greatest popularity. Gathering at the public school grounds (the playground at today's Stuart Wood School), the processions became more spectacular with each passing year. They reached a peak in 1923 and 1924 when 150 automobiles, many of them elaborately decorated, were used to transport hundreds of children down to Riverside Park. The longest parades stretched for nearly three kilometres, and attendance in the park was reported at 3,500 people in 1921 at a time when the population of the city was barely 4,500.

The celebrations of 1920 were particularly notable as the Hudson's Bay Company paid all expenses involved to commemorate the company's 250th anniversary. Cash prizes were offered for the best-decorated floats and automobiles, and proceeds from the evening dance permitted the organising committee to donate nearly $200 to both the Royal Inland Hospital and the Parks Board. The company presented strings of pearls to the queens and maids of honour of 1919 and 1920, and gave a commemorative signet ring and an engraved pencil case to the new queen Jessie MacKay. The manager of the local store authorised a "six-day selling event" and expressed the hope that its generosity in sponsoring the May festival would "be a means of endearing the name of the Company in the hearts of the people." In her address, read by Mr. H.R. Ireland, Queen Jessie stated that the generosity had indeed won a place in the hearts of her subjects, and commended the Hudson's Bay Company "as an eminent example of energy, of resourcefulness and of unfailing loyalty." Though the corporate support was certainly welcome, the May festival had become a genuinely profitable event even without it. Ticket sales for the day's activities and the evening dance typically generated sufficient revenue in the early 1920s to permit donations to both the Royal Inland Hospital and the Parks Board. Even following such donations, the May Day Committee in 1925 began its preparations for the year with a balance of nearly $400 in the bank.

The 1920 May Day also witnessed another change as boys, for the first time since the earliest years of the festival in Kamloops, took part in the plaiting of the maypole. This renewed interest partially explains the increase in the number of maypoles required, from one as late as 1918 to five in 1924—the year in which much excitement was generated by the news that the Fox Film Company planned to film the dances and ceremonies.

Boys enjoyed sporting events and decorating their bicycles.

Courtesy of Joyce Klassen and Don Wilson

Another innovation, dating from the war years, was the obligation of the queen and her maids of honour to pay a visit to the Royal Inland Hospital. The visits were necessarily brief as they occurred between the end of the sports events and the banquet, but the royal party was certainly well received. In 1921, returned soldier patients at RIH insisted that the whole royal party should accompany them to the hospital roof to have photographs taken by Kamloops photographer John Scales. The plaiting of the maypole was repeated for the entertainment of patients at the Tranquille Sanatorium. Also customarily visited were the Sisters of St. Ann's Academy, who welcomed their visitors with a short speech and a bouquet. Their initial opposition to the event evidently waned over the years; in 1925, St. Ann's student Elsie Giddens was one of the candidates for May Queen.

So successful was the Kamloops festival that a number of neighbouring communities launched their own May Day celebrations after the First World War. Both Falkland and Chase began their annual May festivals at this time, and, just across the river, the village of North Kamloops established a separate May Day event in 1921. In order not to conflict with the larger Kamloops festival, the organisers chose to celebrate theirs on the Victoria Day weekend. Throughout the 1920s, the North Kamloops parade would form at Ellsay's store and follow a route to the Home Farm grounds where, courtesy of the British Columbia Fruitlands Company, the sports events and maypole dances occurred. Just as the Rocky Mountain Rangers band had performed at Kamloops' first May Day, so, too, did it lead the first parade in North Kamloops in 1921.

In Kamloops itself, the May festival looked as if it would be an annual event indefinitely. Each year's event was described as the best ever and each drew large and appreciative crowds. A ten-day election campaign for queen in 1925 saw a recount of ballots become necessary as Althea Lynes defeated Kathleen New by just two votes. Ironically, an accident placed Althea in hospital, and Kathleen became queen. Delighted parents saw their favourites plait the four maypoles in singles, doubles, and "spider's web" and watched more than 100 children perform the Danish dance of greeting, the Shoemaker's Dance, the Ace of Diamonds, and

Hickory, Dickory, Dock. An exuberant poem "To the May Queen" appeared in *The Sentinel* and the public school children presented their appreciative queen with a wristwatch. Competition for regal honours became particularly keen in 1926 when nearly thirty candidates came forward. Jean MacKay from Stuart Wood emerged as the winner, following in the footsteps of her sisters Flora and Jessie who had been May Queens in 1911 and 1920 respectively.

In 1927, however, indications appeared that all was not well with the Kamloops May Day. The school board refused to give the usual school holiday, stating that it was no longer willing to interfere with students' learning for such a purpose. The Kamloops festival that year did take place, but it occurred on 24 May, in competition with the regularly scheduled North Kamloops May Day. Though the board did again grant the holiday in 1928 and in the following years, it was not as a result of a united opposition by students, teachers and the public to an unpopular decision such as had occurred twenty years earlier in 1908.

The festivals of 1927, 1928 and 1929 proceeded essentially as usual, with newspaper headlines like "May Day Delights Its Thousands in Smiling Weather" again being typical page-one fare. However, the "annual red letter day in the juvenile calendar" was finding it increasingly difficult to attract juvenile attention. Though many sought to be queen, fewer children—both male and female—were interested in joining in the maypole dances. By 1929, the number of maypoles was reduced to three and once again all the dancers were female, male pupils having become unanimously unwilling to participate. Even the female participants were not so numerous or enthusiastic as in previous years. Difficulty was also experienced in finding teachers and other adults prepared to devote the required amounts of time and energy. Since the early 1920s, the Elks Club's annual Flag Day had become associated with May Day, and perhaps patriotic speeches condemning the ignorance of Kamloops school children about the Union Jack, though well intentioned, were not well calculated to sustain the fragile magic of a children's festival. Whatever the causes, for the first time there was talk of cancellation.

Nevertheless, the supper held in the banquet room of the new Plaza Hotel for the May Queen of 1929 was an elaborate affair:

> *It was a very happy occasion indeed, the band playing in the rotunda, beautiful table decorations of white tull, apple blossom and pale pink tapers. There were favours for all, and pearl chokers for the queen, ex-queen and maids of honour, the gift of the queen's mother.*

Later that evening, an orchestra headed by 1916's May Queen, Lygia Dorion, provided the dance music at the fine new Elks Hall on Seymour Street. The music they played proved to be the swan song for the original Kamloops May festival. The adults of the community had lost interest. When the annual organisational meeting was called to make plans for the May festival of 1930, only six people attended. The festival was immediately cancelled for lack of public interest. The organisers of the North Kamloops May Day experienced a parallel decline in interest, and, in 1930, were able to offer only a limited sports programme of games and races. There would be no May Queen on either shore of the Thompson River in 1930 or 1931.

As might be expected after nearly thirty years of a public event, there was much nostalgia expressed in the local community for the children's festival. The Athletic Association stepped forward to revive May Day with considerable success in 1932 and 1933. Each school nominated its candidate for May Queen, with the winner's name being drawn from a hat. Half-day holidays were again declared, royal visits were made to the Tranquille Sanatorium and to the children's ward at RIH, banquets were held at the Leland Hotel, and dances took place at the Athletic Association Hall. The parade of 1933 was said to be the longest ever for a May Day celebration.

However, the energetic Kamloops Athletic Association also sponsored a May 24th celebration in 1933, with horse racing events at the East End Park, a baseball game versus Revelstoke, and tickets for a car draw. There was the ubiquitous Rocky Mountain Rangers band, a concert, a dance and a parade, and, with the crowning of a nineteen-year-old festival queen, the day must have seemed to some an adult parody of a familiar children's theme. In 1934 an attempt was made to combine the adult and children's festivities on the May 24th weekend. There was a dance around a single maypole and 250 children performed a flag drill. The attempt was not repeated. Kamloops saw no more May festivals during the 1930s.

The last May Queen of the 1930s, Gertrude Rigby poses with her entourage in 1933.
Kamloops Museum and Archives photograph number 1523

Renewed interest in a children's May festival emerged just at the end of the Second World War, as the community sought to return to a simpler era. As early as 1945, North Kamloops, Brocklehurst and Westsyde jointly organised a children's celebration with a maypole, a banquet, sports events and an evening dance. Queen Mary Krehel also visited the residents at Tranquille. Not to be outdone, the Kamloops Lions Club announced its intention to hold a May Day festival in 1946, but was forced to cancel when it realised that the organisational requirements were beyond its reach. Club members did travel to New Westminster to learn from organisers there.

However, the revival of the Kamloops May Day festival that occurred so successfully in 1947 was achieved not by the Lions Club. Once again, the Kamloops Fire Department took responsibility. This time reaching beyond their own ranks, they involved interested individuals and the parent-teacher associations of the city schools, and set to work to revive all the plans and procedures of the 1920s. Fire department members rescued the maypoles from beneath the grandstand at Riverside Park. Teachers at the Junior High School, Stuart Wood, Lloyd George, Fruitlands, St. Ann's, and the Kamloops Indian Residential School all agreed to take part. On May 16th, thirteen-year-old Iona Hudson became the city's first children's May Queen since 1933.

The very windy May Day of 1948 was notable for a number of reasons. The Kamloops School District declared May 17th an official school holiday to accommodate the children's festival. Governor-General Viscount and Lady Alexander, who were in Kamloops on an official tour visiting the hospital, Paul Lake, Valleyview and the Tranquille Sanatorium, took part in the May Day ceremonies. At the special invitation of the organising committee, six former May Queens were present. Olive McLean (1913) and Jean Campbell (1927) still lived in Kamloops, but Laura McCall (1917) and Alma Horne (1922) travelled from Victoria, and Betty Corbould (1932) came from Winnipeg. Also present was the only former queen who had been unable to attend the ceremonies back in 1915—Violet Kyle (1904) travelled from Vancouver to be part of the festivities in 1948.

They would all have been pleased had they returned the following year to see nearly 2,000 children take part in the activities of the festival of 1949. They would all have been saddened to learn that, despite its apparent success, the Kamloops May Day ended abruptly in 1949, leaving even fewer clues about its demise than its original predecessor had done in 1929. Sadly reminiscent of the organising committee's announcement of twenty years earlier, the only trace of a May Day in 1950 in the newspapers of the day is the report of its cancellation due to "insufficient interest."

The early 1950s saw the emergence in May of the first Miss Kamloops competitions, but those cannot be said to be descendants of the Fire Laddies' May Day of 1903. The Kamloops May Day festivities initially were based upon magic and innocence. Perhaps their disappearance is explained by realising how difficult it was in the twentieth century to sustain magic and innocence. Perhaps somehow the city had simply outgrown the event. It is interesting to compare the appearance of the post-Second World War queens with their pre-First World War counterparts. The photographs from the early part of the century show us the faces of children; the royal parties of the late 1940s appear much more mature.

As difficult as it is to understand why the children's May Day disappeared so abruptly, it is even more difficult to imagine today what the day meant to its participants at the time. Pearl Chapman, five years after she had been crowned May Queen of 1923, wrote: "There is no real definition for the fete; May Day is just May Day and a law unto herself." But maybe the secret was clearly revealed in a "retirement speech" of 1933. Before she surrendered her crown, outgoing May Queen Betty Corbould advised all her youthful and loyal subjects:

[Today] forget the shadows on the dial, and be what you are still in heart—just laughter-loving happy children. Lay aside dull care, for surely it has no place amid the flowers of May.

May Queens of Kamloops

1903 Edith Lee
1904 Violet Kyle
1905 Mary Barnhart
1906 Beatrice Allen
1907 Jessie McDonald
1908 Annie Noble
1909 Maud Kelly
1910 Irene Irwin
1911 Flora MacKay
1912 Elizabeth Robinson
1913 Olive McLean
1914 Hilda McCrum
1915 Jean Harper
1916 Lygia Dorion
1917 Laura McCall
1918 Reta McLean
1919 Helen Blair
1920 Jessie MacKay
1921 Jean Miller
1922 Alma Home
1923 Pearl Chapman
1924 Annie Lytle
1925 Kathleen New
1926 Jean MacKay
1927 Jean Campbell
1928 Pearl Nell
1929 Dorothy Churchill
1930 and 1931 cancelled
1932 Betty Corbould
1933 Gertrude Rigby
1947 Iona Hudson
1948 Doris Evans
1949 Donna Johnson

May Queens of North Kamloops

1921	Lillie Farquharson	1926	Alice Willie
1922	Edna Nixon	1927	Alice McKnight
1923	Jean Wyse	1928	Rose Nicholson
1924	Rosemary Williams	1929	Faith McKnight
1925	Louise Emmerick		

1945 Mary Krehel

1947 Elsie Schimpf

A retiring May Queen crowns her successor.

Courtesy of Rein Stamm

Tranquille: No Stranger to Controversy

In November 1907, British Columbia's first hospital for the treatment of tuberculosis opened near the mouth of Tranquille Creek. By that date, the creek—often referred to as Tranquille River—had been subjected to the devastating practice of hydraulic mining and had suffered changes to its course as miners fought Nature in their search for gold. Today the creek runs freely, and the buildings erected for the institution that came to be known as the Tranquille Sanatorium stand silent and abandoned alongside those constructed for the Mental Health operation that succeeded it. In various states of decay, these structures have long been waiting for a development proposal to provide a purposeful future for a property that has lacked one for nearly three decades. Controversies and myths have surrounded the property at Tranquille for well over a hundred years. Some of these controversies survive only historically, without resonance except in the narratives of their time; others remain current and stubbornly persistent. They shape popular beliefs about what existed and occurred at Tranquille in the past and they influence opinions about what should take place there today.

Early Days—Early Controversies

In the 1890s, the proposal to establish a facility for treatment of tuberculosis was received with much initial enthusiasm in Kamloops. Just a few years later, however, when such an institution had become a practical possibility, almost the entire community of Kamloops seemed united in opposition. Both the local newspapers objected to the location in Kamloops of a treatment facility and painted a picture of plague and pestilence. Politicians and business leaders raged against the notion, sending petitions and delegations to Victoria to leave the provincial government in no doubt about their opinion on the matter. Opponents went so far as to point out the negative effects of the prevailing dust and winds at Kamloops. At the same time they praised the attributes of rival communities and launched personal attacks against the scheme's chief proponent, provincial medical health officer John Fagan.

Because of the opposition, the British Columbia Anti-tuberculosis Society abandoned its initial plans for construction at the foot of Batchelor Hill, but was determined to locate a sanatorium to take advantage of the beneficial air of the Dry Belt. After some skilful speeches and lobbying of local political figures by Dr. Fagan, the notion that a sanatorium could be built "near but not in Kamloops" was accepted by most of those previously hostile to the scheme. A delegation from the Anti-tuberculosis Society visited several sites along the shores of Kamloops Lake in the summer of 1907, guided by local alderman and real estate agent John Robinson. Impressed by the ranch of William and Jane Fortune, arrangements were made to purchase the property. Within a few short months, renovations of the Fortune ranch houses were complete, staff had been hired, and British Columbia's first tuberculosis sanatorium admitted its first patients on 28 November 1907.

Several controversies erupted almost immediately. Dr. Fagan was involved in the nasty dispute between the Fortunes and John Robinson, who apparently had been acting as their sales agent at the time of the delegation's visit and was suing for his commission. The business relationship between the Fortunes and Robinson had been concealed from Fagan; nevertheless, he was required to testify at the court proceedings. The sanatorium reached full capacity just a month after opening and began to deny admission to prospective patients. There were allegations of poor quality food, the effectiveness of medical treatments was questioned, and staff accommodations were found to be inadequate. Though stretched financially, the Anti-tuberculosis Society was obliged to plan to expand its facilities at Tranquille in order to qualify for continued financial assistance from the provincial government, and was shocked when it was denied charitable status by the federal government.

While the Tranquille institution had no choice but to accept patients in advanced stages of the disease, Dr. Irving, the medical superintendent at Tranquille, began to treat less serious cases privately, despite the objections of his employer. The dispute with the board of the Anti-tuberculosis Society led to his dismissal early in 1910. A few months later he publicly accused the administration of Tranquille of mismanagement and incompetence and opened his own facility, accepting only patients who could pay and who were in the earliest and most easily treated stages of the disease. The local community was not pleased with the prospect of a significant jump in the local tubercular population, and as the mud was flung from all sides, largely overlooked was the fact that a "two-tier' system of tuberculosis treatment had become available in the Kamloops region.

The main building at Tranquille in early stages of construction.
Kamloops Museum and Archives photograph number 2000

A series of minor crises and a succession of short-lived administrators provided grist for the mills of the institution's critics. Renamed the King Edward Sanatorium in 1911, Tranquille enjoyed a brief period of stability under the competent administration of Dr. Charles Vrooman, though the society continued to struggle with inadequate financial resources. As the war in Europe dragged on, federal funding became available to finance the treatment of soldier patients suffering from tuberculosis. Soldiers began arriving at Tranquille in late 1915 and, in short order, began to generate the next series of controversies to engulf Tranquille.

When Dr. Vrooman expelled three soldiers for an unauthorised visit to the bars of Kamloops, they responded with allegations that the superintendent was pro-German. An investigation by a former superintendent dismissed this and other spurious charges and recommended that military patients be placed under military command. The recommendation echoed those being made at other institutions across Canada in response to attempts to treat undisciplined soldier-patients.

When the federal and provincial governments combined to finance the construction of new buildings at Tranquille, the numbers of soldier-patients there increased sharply. Another round of soldier discontent led to the resignation of a new superintendent. In a more constructive mode, soldier-patients at Tranquille in the years immediately following the war began the organisation that would eventually become known as the TB Vets.

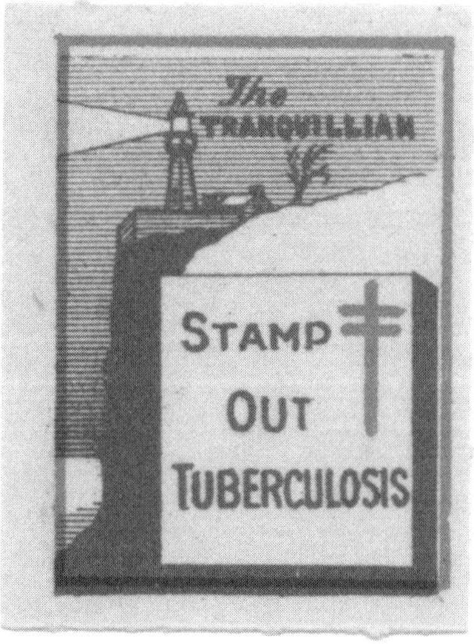

The first Christmas seal in British Columbia was issued at Tranquille in 1926.

The financial inability of the Anti-tuberculosis Society to operate the sanatorium was finally acknowledged by the provincial government when it took over the operation of Tranquille in 1921. The change in responsibility led to a welcome infusion of funds, but also resulted in the new charge that employment and construction contracts at Tranquille were dependent upon political partisanship. With Liberals in power for most of the 1920s, provincial Conservatives frequently claimed that favouritism resulted in Liberals being appointed to positions at Tranquille. When the Conservatives took power in 1928, they launched an investigation of operations at Tranquille that resulted in little change other than the dismissal of several known Liberal supporters. The Liberal return to power in 1933 saw the dismissal of Conservative-appointed employees. As a government-run institution, Tranquille was open to manipulation for political purposes by governing parties, and to allegations from opposition politicians of unfair hiring practices, under funding, and/or extravagant spending. Whether the charges of the moment had

Maturing gardens made Tranquille a local "beauty spot" by the 1920s.

substance or were purely opportunistic, Tranquille would never again be able to dispel lingering suspicions that politics largely determined decisions pertaining to it.

As the institution matured, its routines and processes developed a sort of "natural order" that caused some observers to suggest it was being run almost as a separate little kingdom, with separation from Kamloops too pronounced and social stratification too distinct. A concerned provincial government directed its new superintendent in 1937 to reverse both trends. The success of this new direction is measured by the surviving memoirs of former patients and former employees, the fond recollections their children had of life "at the san", and the attitude of the people of Kamloops to the institution—all of which were generally positive during the 1940s and 1950s.

Controversies did not disappear. The sale of the entire beef herd in the early 1940s met with much local disapproval, as did the initial employment of Japanese farm labourers in the late 1940s. The 1950s saw the renewal of environmental concerns and a call for action on the "deplorable situation" of sewage treatment at Tranquille. The provincial government finally installed a three-acre stabilization pond on the old horse meadow by the lakeshore in March 1957. However, it did not operate satisfactorily due to faulty construction. Both the chronic shortage of nurses and the formation of a local of the BC Government Employees' Union caused management unwelcome stress and strain, but the Tranquille institution was operating in the 1950s just as the

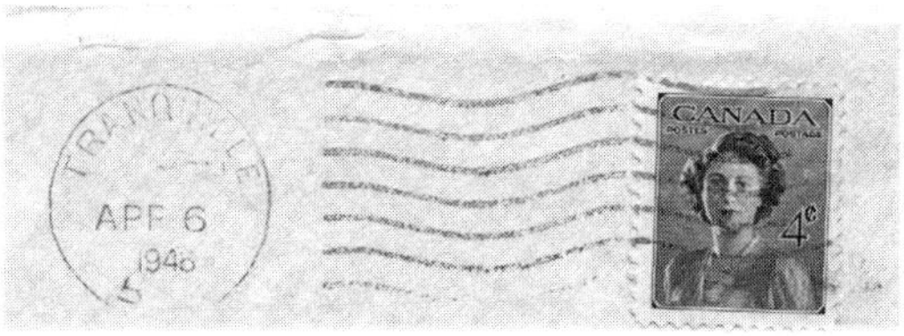

Reading and writing were always popular activities.

founders of the Anti-tuberculosis Society had hoped when they opened it five decades earlier—as an efficient and properly funded facility for the care and treatment of tubercular patients.

An Ending and a Beginning

The success of drug treatments for tuberculosis made it apparent that the institution was nearing the end of its life, and it was surrounding its closure that Tranquille's greatest controversy occurred. The Main Building and the East Pavilion were closed in 1956 amidst rumours—soon discounted—that the site was being considered for use as a federal penitentiary. The people of Kamloops debated the merits of a range of proposals to convert the institution to a new purpose. It soon became apparent that they were as reluctant to see Tranquille close in the 1950s as they had been to see it open in 1907. Should it become an agricultural college or a retirement home, a hospital for the chronically or mentally ill, an art college or a vocational school? One Kamloops council member expressed the fear that Tranquille was about to become a "white elephant."

Finally, the provincial government announced the facility would close by December 1958. The provincial health minister feared that the community of Kamloops was "seething" over the issue of the institution's future, but local MLA Phil Gaglardi privately told sanatorium employees they had no cause to worry. Letters from nurses and former patients in support of keeping the facility open began to appear in *The Sentinel.* The Kamloops Board of Trade urged the government to use the facility for "mental defectives" and sponsored a petition that garnered 1,700 signatures. Local business owners sent telegrams to Premier W.A.C. Bennett urging the continuance of the facility in one form or another, and the Kamloops School Board proposed the use of the site as a vocational college.

Tranquille's one-room schoolhouse in the 1940s.

Gaglardi issued an official statement that the buildings would be used by the government "for some purpose," that most employees would be able to keep their jobs, and that a government committee was examining the options. At the same time, remaining patients were being transferred to Vancouver's Pearson Hospital. Transfers of individual employees to other provincial departments accelerated, and declining student enrolment required the closure of the Tranquille School at the end of June.

The local uproar began to attract attention in the lower mainland. The *Vancouver Sun* sent columnist Elmore Philpott to Tranquille in early June "to find out what the fuss and fury was all about." What he found, evidently to his surprise, was "a whole little city by itself." He noted that the hospital, with its attendant fire hall, power plant, laundry and farm, could treat not just 351 tuberculosis patients, but 351 patients of any variety. Philpott wrote that the institution would be very expensive to start up again if it were allowed to close, and concluded that "every intelligent man, woman and child in Kamloops was determined not to let this great social crime come to pass."

Over the course of the summer, a political storm raged as Gaglardi made contradictory statements that tried the patience of sanatorium employees and the Board of Trade. Finally, in September 1958, the provincial health minister announced that the facilities at Tranquille would be used as a home for "mentally defective" adults between twenty and forty years old who were not a risk to the community. The new patients were to be transferred from overcrowded facilities at Woodlands in the lower mainland. By the terms of the government takeover of 1921, the facility at Tranquille should have been used only for the treatment of tuberculosis, so the proposal to operate a home for mentally challenged adults was contrary to law. Successors to the British Columbia Anti-tuberculosis Society raised no objections to the proposal. They wanted the buildings at Tranquille put to humanitarian use and, with the defeat of tuberculosis apparently assured, released the government from the legal requirement.

Employees were formally advised that the institution would close on 4 October, but Gaglardi immediately found himself embroiled in another controversy with the remaining sanatorium employees, who were still wondering what their fate was to be. With no assurances of employment after 4 October and ineligible for unemployment insurance as employees of the provincial government, they remained unconvinced by Gaglardi's promise that the first patients would arrive "sometime in October." The sense of unease was further enhanced when a prominent local Social Credit supporter with no administrative background was appointed superintendent at Tranquille. The first Mental Health residents finally arrived at Tranquille in July 1959, ending a process which had caused much unnecessary confusion and which had tarnished what should have been an optimistic beginning to a new chapter in the life of the facilities at Tranquille.

Tranquille Farm and School

The new institution grew rapidly over the course of the next few years, accepting people with mild and more severe mental handicaps as well as those with cerebral palsy. By the late 1960s, the combined population of staff and patients at Tranquille was equal to that of the sanatorium at its peak. For its first decade, the institution enjoyed a period relatively free from controversy, though questions about political interference in hiring and debates about the most appropriate methods of treatment and care were frequently heard. The decade of the 1970s saw an increasing acceptance of the view that institutionalisation was not in the best interests of the patient population at places like Tranquille, and the announcement by the provincial government that Tranquille would be phased out by the end of the 1980s surprised few observers.

Even before that announcement, the administration at Tranquille had developed programmes and policies to return selected patients to community surroundings. It was a course of action that renewed controversy in Kamloops as some neighbourhoods objected to the placement of group homes in their locations. However, the level of controversy was minor compared to the storm that soon followed. In the early summer of 1983, the provincial government introduced a sweeping programme of restraint and declared its intention to eliminate the jobs of thousands of provincial employees. The Ministry of Human Resources—by then the department responsible for Tranquille—announced that the closure of the facility at Tranquille would be sharply accelerated and that, as part of the restraint programme, the first provincial employees to be laid off in British Columbia would be some of those working at the Tranquille Farm.

The cluster of legislation that comprised the restraint programme therefore took on particular resonance with both the employees and the administration at Tranquille. As the broad implications of the government's intentions became more apparent, members of the BC Government Employees' Union employed at Tranquille decided that only dramatic action could convey the depth of their concern. In mid July, union members declared Tranquille "occupied" and took over the administration and other buildings. Assuming responsibility for all aspects of the operation at Tranquille, the BCGEU declared that if government could disregard contracts, so could government employees. The occupation lasted three full weeks before the union merged its efforts with the broader Solidarity movement that was sweeping the province. Public opinion concerning the occupation divided predictably. Government supporters were enraged by the illegal action; Solidarity supporters saw the occupation as justifiable, almost heroic.

Though the government and Solidarity reached an arrangement in November, the timetable for the accelerated closure was not changed. The Tranquille School and Farm were to close by the end of 1985. During its last eighteen months of operation, the institution faced the occupation and was behind picket lines on two separate occasions. It was responsible for preparing its resident patients for their transition to community living in far less time than most of them reasonably required. Despite everything, the staff met all obligations.

The final controversy of Tranquille School and Farm should have been that its management and employees received so little public recognition of the magnitude of their achievement. However, the recent distribution of a "common experience payment" to former residents of Tranquille has added an unexpected footnote and a considerable amount of misunderstanding. The payment by the BC Institutional Legacy Trust Fund is intended only as "a goodwill gesture" in recognition that difficulties were experienced by some residents at Tranquille and its sister institutions. It is not to be interpreted to imply that abuse is alleged.

Padova and Post-Padova

For several years following the second closure of Tranquille, the property again patiently awaited its future. With the benefit of expensive upgrades completed even while the institution was preparing to close, it was generally thought that new options for Tranquille would soon be announced. All the possibilities discussed at the time of the first shutdown resurfaced. Several options seemed promising. Time passed. The City of Kamloops reluctantly footed the bill for fire protection and police services as trespassing, pilfering and partying became increasingly common. Most people in Kamloops simply looked forward to the day when the complex—in whatever new guise seemed most feasible—would once again contribute to the local economy. Still nothing happened. The provincial government finally admitted it had no plans for development and put the property on the market in 1988.

For nearly three years afterwards there were no takers. Finally, to much applause from Kamloops, Giovanni Camporese from Vancouver purchased the property and announced plans to establish a multi-faceted destination resort. Some skepticism was felt about the practicality of the plans when it was learned that ostrich races were considered a real possibility, and considerable dismay was expressed when Camporese renamed the property Padova City after his hometown in Italy. However, there was general satisfaction that the facilities at Tranquille were to be put to good use at last. But by 1995, with no development taking place and with mortgage obligations not being met, optimism evaporated. The grounds and buildings were seen to be deteriorating rapidly. A reluctant provincial government resumed ownership in 1998 and, in lieu of taxes, subsequently passed Padova/Tranquille to an equally reluctant City of Kamloops.

After much legal machination—including a decision by the Supreme Court of Canada—the property was acquired by Ed

Nielsen's B.C. Wilderness Tours in May 2001. Once more the announced plans were dramatic and extensive, but the vision and energy of Nielsen made it seem likely that the property had a viable future once more. Nielsen accomplished a great deal in a short time, but his untimely death in 2002 again cast a shadow over Tranquille's future prospects.

There have also been shadows cast over Tranquille's past. Partly due to the nature of its two institutional periods—as a tuberculosis hospital and as a facility for people with mental and physical disabilities—partly to the property's long period of abandonment, and partly to the decrepit appearance of the buildings, the history and the purposes served at Tranquille are widely (and often wilfully) misrepresented. The more gullible believe that the tunnels connecting the main buildings were constructed for sinister purposes, that the facility housed an insane asylum, was subsequently used for genetic research, and is currently haunted by the ghosts of those tormented there over the years. Some young people trespass and convince themselves they are "invading" what they describe as a "freaky farm." And, in the belief that its musical style reflects Tranquille's imagined dark currents, a local band has named itself after the site. Though the Internet did not invent these notions, it is used to spread them and has added satanic and extra-terrestrial elements to the mix.

So what of the future of Tranquille? That is a question that has been asked locally—at times urgently—for more than a century. Promising to preserve some elements of the site's history, the current owners recently proposed to develop the property for mixed residential and recreational use. The proposal generated the latest in the series of controversies surrounding Tranquille. Environmental concerns were raised and the British Columbia Agricultural Land Commission initially rejected the plan on the grounds that agricultural land should not be used for a golf course. However, a modified proposal has recently been accepted and Tranquille is once again on the verge of significant change. It was only a matter of time before some sort of practical vision for the future of Tranquille met with acceptance. The greatest controversy now is that the property has remained unused and undeveloped for so long.

Recommended Reading

For the story of gold mining at Tranquille, see Eldon Graham's "Treasure at Tranquille" in *Reflections: Thompson Valley Histories* (Plateau Press, 1994). For the tuberculosis years at Tranquille, see *A Whole Little City by Itself: Tranquille and Tuberculosis* (Plateau Press, 1999). For the operation of Tranquille School and Farm and the BCGEU actions, see Gena Crowston's *The Ghosts of Tranquille Past* (self-published, 2002).

Mary Spencer and Bill Miner: Memory and Legacy in Local History

Mary Spencer and Bill Miner have become essential components of the local historical narrative. It seems that accounts of Kamloops history are no longer complete without reference to Mary and Bill. Though most local residents are generally aware of the historical realities concerning the pair, the story as it is commonly presented—especially to tourists—links Miner and Spencer in an impossible folkloric tale of robbery and romance. In film, music and print, their alleged relationship is explored as a romantic sidebar that is increasingly important to the ongoing celebration of the personality cult that surrounds the train robber Bill Miner.

Bill Miner is a celebrity. Of that there can be little doubt. His exploits survive in a sanitized version of events that has attracted interest for over one hundred years. The story has begun to morph into a tale no longer expected to be grounded in the realities of local history. Mary Spencer is not a celebrity, but a character based upon her has become an important embellishment to the Miner legend. While the fabricated Bill Miner narrative serves to redeem his character from the realities of a criminal and manipulative life, the same narrative obscures the achievements of Mary Spencer and deflects attention from the significant role she played in the early artistic life of the city of Kamloops. Perhaps the modern fictionalised representation of both Mary Spencer and Bill Miner can be enjoyed even more if, at the same time, the realities of their lives are also considered.

Mary Spencer

Little is known of the details of Mary Spencer's life before, during, or after her stay in Kamloops. Her parents, Abraham and Margaret Spencer, emigrated with their son and daughter from England in the mid 1850s, settling in Dunnville, Ontario. A second daughter, Mary, was born in 1857 and a third, Isobel, four years later. Abraham Spencer apparently abandoned the family in 1862. Soon afterwards Margaret, seeking better educational opportunities for her children, moved with them to St. Catharines. It was there that Isobel developed her interest in horticulture and Mary her talents as an artist and photographer. Perhaps to pursue business opportunities in their chosen fields, Isobel and Mary moved with their mother to Port Colborne in 1890. A large painting by her graced the archway of the original Baptist church there until the building was remodelled circa 1930, and her pen and ink sketch of a nephew is still held by the museum at Port Colborne.

Photograph of Mrs. Mitchell by Mary Spencer.
Kamloops Museum and Archives photograph number 4421

Whatever may have been the ambitions

Photograph of Nettie Smith by Mary Spencer.
Kamloops Museum and Archives photograph number 105

that took the family to that community, they apparently remained unfulfilled. Over eighty years of age in 1899, Mrs. Spencer decided to accompany her two unmarried daughters as they moved again—this time much further—to Kamloops in British Columbia. Very soon after they arrived, Mary opened a photographic studio and also began to offer lessons in oil painting. The only photographer in the Thompson region at the time, her studio catered on the local demand for individual and family portraits, and she is known to have scheduled trips to Ashcroft to photograph residents in that community as well.

In the decade that the Spencer sisters lived and worked in Kamloops, they left remarkably little upon which to construct an assessment of their lives here. It appears that Mary was the chief bread-winner for the family. Isobel is identified as a "tailoress" in the census return of 1901, but opened her own horticultural business soon afterwards—a decision that could suggest household expenses were not being met by Mary's income alone. Mary served on the executive of the local Women's Christian Temperance Union and is thought to have been deeply committed to the then strict moral outlook of the Baptist Church to which all three women belonged. After the death of their mother, the two sisters continued to live and work in Kamloops until the end of the decade when they made what proved to be their final move, this time to Summerland in the Okanagan.

With so little to contradict imagination, this paucity of factual evidence about her life is what allows authors and film makers to speculate so freely upon what Mary Spencer's motives and feelings may have been. And the sole reason she has become the object of this speculation is the fact that she took photographs of three men who were captured soon after they botched an attempt to hold up a train at Ducks, just a few miles east of Kamloops, in May 1906. One of the three bandits was Bill Miner.

Through a combination of her own initiative, the requirements of the superintendent of the Provincial Police, and subsequent individual requests, she photographed those accused of the robbery at Ducks and those involved in the capture of the fugitives near Douglas Lake a few days later. Under exclusive contract to the *Vancouver Province*, she was later also permitted to photograph the proceedings of the preliminary hearing at the Kamloops courthouse. Because of that contract with the *Vancouver Province*, the superintendent of Provincial Police needed the permission of the newspaper to have Mary Spencer—the only photographer in the Kamloops region in 1906—take photographs of the accused for circulation to potential witnesses throughout southern British Columbia and the American west.

With newspapers in Canada and the United States falling over themselves for copies of the photographs of Miner and his cohorts, Mary Spencer suddenly enjoyed the prospect of a significant financial gain. The Provincial Police quickly scuttled that possibility. The superintendent advised her that the publication of the photographs could jeopardise a fair trial and insisted that, as the photographs were taken for police purposes, they were not available for sale or distribution by either her or the *Vancouver Province.* Before the police ban was imposed, however, the now famous images were published by the *Province* and the *Kamloops Standard.* In the process, Mary Spencer had become the first woman, probably in the British Empire, to take official photographs of individuals accused of a crime.

Mary Spencer's chief reward for taking the photographs of Bill Miner has been to provide the romantic interest for him in fictionalised representations of his life. She is the basis of the character Kate in the highly regarded film *The Grey Fox.* The Two River Junction Musical Review, a local production popular with tourists travelling on the Rocky Mountaineer, presents Mary Spencer as a local reporter trying to capture the story of the train robbery who finds instead "that Billy has captured her heart." Neither production pretends to tell its audience that it is presenting them with a historically accurate account, and most people are aware that fact and fiction are being mixed for entertainment purposes, but few will take the time to determine which details are true and which are not. It is surprising how quickly fiction becomes accepted as fact. When a class of high school students was asked recently if any of them had heard of Mary Spencer, one student answered quickly. "Yes," he said, "Bill Miner's girlfriend." Other students nodded in agreement.

Mary Spencer does not deserve to be remembered as "Bill Miner's girlfriend." There is nothing in the historical record to suggest such a possibility and no historian has ever characterised her that way. The emerging popular belief that she was involved romantically with Bill Miner is simply another indication of the power of entertainment media to influence opinion even at a purely regional or local level. It is a belief that has developed in spite of—not because of—the extensive historical research into the Bill Miner legend.

Photographs of Bill Miner and his accomplices by Mary Spencer.
Courtesy of Don Stewart

So what are the facts? Fundamentally, there is only one—she did take photographs of Bill Miner. The photographs taken by her at the Kamloops gaol provide us with the most widely known and most extensively reproduced photographs of the Miner gang. They also provide a clear indication of Spencer's skill as a portrait photographer. Essentially mug shots, the images are obviously superior to similar photographs of the same subjects taken elsewhere. Without them, we would have only the inferior prison photographs of Miner taken earlier at Alcatraz and later at the penitentiaries in New Westminster and Gainesville, Georgia. Perhaps, therefore, Mary Spencer has only herself to blame for the speculation that now surrounds her. The photographs she took of Miner are the ones that truly invite viewers to look more closely and to speculate about the character of the man behind those famous eyes. Many who accept the invitation convince themselves that they see a kindly and admirable individual, a man who needed only love to set him straight...love from a morally solid lady friend...just like, well...just like Mary Spencer.

Fantasy aside, it is as a skilful portrait photographer that Spencer does deserve to be remembered. She left a historical record of photographs of individuals and families who were residents of Kamloops and environs during the first decade of the last century. That legacy alone is sufficient to earn the gratitude of those interested in local history. But Spencer's photographs provide more than just a chronicle. When compared to the work of her contemporaries in Kamloops and elsewhere, her photography distinguishes itself. Though landscapes were also amongst her subjects, it is her portrait photography that is particularly remarkable, revealing character and personality to an extent that was rare in the photography of the day. It can only be hoped that her photographic legacy will one day be presented in a retrospective exhibition of her work, perhaps with an accompanying publication. A greater recognition of the life and work of Mary Spencer—in a historically accurate fashion—would surely find an appreciative wider audience.

Photograph of Kamloops and the Thompson valley by Mary Spencer.
Kamloops Museum and Archives photograph number 876

Bill Miner

Bill Miner is well known in Kamloops. For years his image stared out at passers-by from a huge banner in front of the museum. Few local histories fail to feature him; pubs and cafes and tourist attractions draw attention to him. His name is familiar to school children and, were he alive today, it is not inconceivable he could be elected to public office—not solely because of the strong recognition factor, but also because he is widely perceived to have been a nice guy. Kamloops has long invested a great deal in the figure of Bill Miner as a tourist attraction, and a "Miner for Mayor" campaign would attract at least an initial interest. On the other hand, perhaps people would come to realise (and save the present author from continuing with this absurd historical fantasy) that, once elected, Bill Miner would not hesitate to rob the electorate blind. Based on everything we know about him, it seems he would betray their trust with every opportunity that presented a personal advantage to him.

The details of Miner's early life have long been a matter for speculation, largely because he lied about himself at every opportunity. However, meticulous research by local historian Peter Grauer has managed to establish the essential facts. Miner was his surname, but his first name was Ezra. He was born in the state of Michigan in 1846, moving with the rest of his family to California following the death of his father about a decade later. As a young man, he began to pursue a generally unsuccessful career as a horse thief and a robber of stage coaches. Rarely able to elude the long arm of the law following his misadventures, Miner spent most of his youth and middle age incarcerated.

Released from prison in 1901, Bill Miner at the age of 55 was a man desperately in need of a career change. So he turned from robbing stagecoaches to robbing trains. After his first attempt in Oregon failed miserably, he crossed into Canada to try his hand with the Canadian Pacific Railway Company, and, near Mission in 1904, Miner achieved one of his rare successes. He and his gang escaped with a considerable amount of loot. With that robbery, Bill Miner became an instant celebrity in Canada. This was partially due to the exceptional interest people in the early years of the twentieth century had in tales of the Wild West. In print publications and silent movies, fact merged with fiction to make folk heroes of outlaws such as Belle Starr, Jesse James and Billy the Kid. The robbery at Ducks nearly two years later, despite its failure, seemed to confirm Miner's right to membership in the club. His subsequent career of imprisonment, escape, failed robberies and more imprisonment added sufficient colourful detail to his biography that he is remembered today nearly a century after his death in 1913.

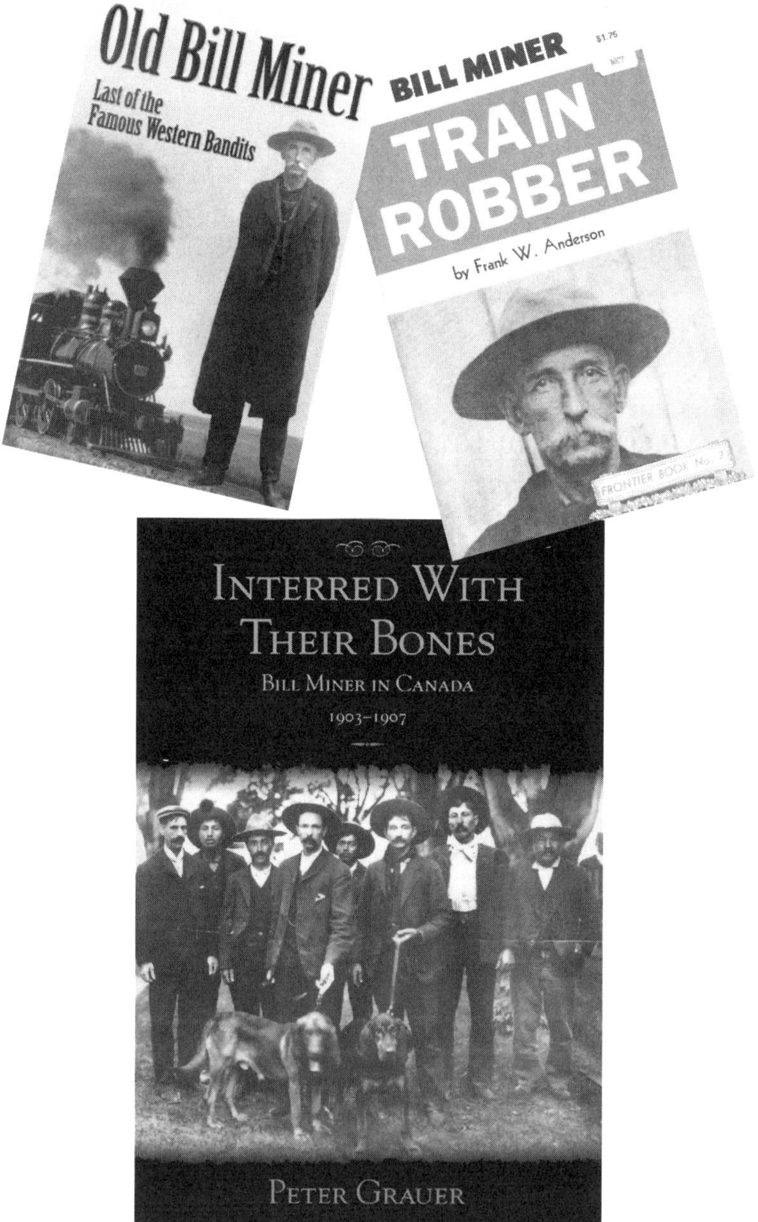

Covers of books about Bill Miner invariably use Mary Spencer photographs.
Courtesy of Heritage House Publishing and Peter Grauer

However, an examination of the facts of Bill Miner's career reveals a character that presents little to admire. As a thief, he seems to be more of a comic figure than anything else. He was inept and would often overlook obvious items of value in his robberies; he could get lost making his escapes; he would misjudge the character of both victims and associates; he spent almost all his adult life in prison. Even when they were well planned, his robberies yielded treasure more by chance than by design—if they yielded any treasure at all. The potential for violence was always present. During one episode in the United States in 1882, he may have shot two lawmen; if he did not, his partners certainly did. With little apparent regret, he left a fiancée in Michigan at the altar. From his Canadian base at Princeton, he smuggled drugs and illegal immigrants across the border from Washington State. Allegations of his probable racism and opium use now seem well established.

This is hardly a resume to make a mother proud. And it is certainly not the substance of the Bill Miner promoted locally. Ours is the Bill Miner of fiction, almost of cartoons. He is a benign character, celebrated for his gentlemanly manners and charm, for his courage in standing against the much resented Canadian Pacific Railway Company, and for having brought a taste of the lawless Wild West to a region proud of its own otherwise law abiding western heritage. He is a celebrity manufactured for tourist consumption, and we soften the reality of the historical Miner wherever possible, often referring to him with the diminutive Billy (which sounds friendlier than Bill or William) and ignoring the fact that he kept company with prostitutes as we provide him with a respectable love interest more consistent with the reputation of a gentleman.

The local Bill Miner story has an element of Zorro or Batman about it. Here's the plot: an unsuspecting population has amongst them an individual who arouses no suspicion whatsoever that he may be anything other than he seems to be. As occasion demands—for Zorro and Batman, to fight evil; for Miner, to rob trains or steal horses—the *alter ego* emerges, conducts himself briefly in a fashion completely at odds with his mundane existence, and returns to his everyday identity just in time to escape detection. The most obvious difference is that for Miner a change of costume was not required. The most significant difference is that, while Zorro and Batman fought oppression on behalf of a deceived and helpless populace, Miner pursued a criminal career while deceiving the local population.

In fact, this is where Bill Miner's real talents lay—not as a stagecoach and train robber, but as a con artist. He duped people by a superficial geniality and generosity—tipping his hat, buying drinks, handing out small change and presents to children. The real loot was reserved for his benefit alone. People today seem to focus upon the geniality, admire the successful deception of honest citizens, and minimize the crimes committed. In the phrase commonly used to identify him—the gentleman bandit—the word gentleman is emphasized, while the word bandit is ignored or seen only in an essentially harmless Robin Hood kind of context. In fiction, he is a kind and generous neighbour. One published version of his career states that after a woman had been robbed by Bill Miner, she may have been poorer, but she also found herself a little in love. The title of the film *The Grey Fox* for distribution in the United Kingdom was changed to *The Robber Who'll Steal your Heart*. It's almost as if Miner had to shake off the women before he could safely escape with what he had stolen from them.

The fact that truth is exceptionally difficult to establish in history does not mean that all versions of history are equally valid. There are two competing versions of Bill Miner as a historical figure. One presents him as kind, generous to children, thoughtful, charming, polite especially to the ladies, wise, and, despite the gun in his hand, generally harmless—the sort of guy everyone would welcome as a neighbour. This is the legendary Bill

Miner we prefer to present to our visitors—a presentation that is designed as entertainment rather than remembrance. The second version is not entirely the antithesis of the first, but recognises that the face Miner presented to the world was meant not only to deceive, but also to conceal a hardened and unrepentant criminal. I prefer the second Bill Miner. Of course, he is far less likeable—and, no, I would not want him living next door in this guise—but he is also more complex, more of a real person when we acknowledge that the substance of his character contradicts the veneer placed upon it.

Mary and Bill

Folklore captivates the imagination. It usually manages to appeal across generations and the best stories will survive changing tastes and the test of time. We are fortunate to be able to watch a local folkloric tale developing. As embellishments are added, the story takes twists and turns and generates songs, poetry, serious studies and fantasies. By all means, let us enjoy the fictions and entertainments, but, at the same time, let us not lose sight of the historic Bill Miner and Mary Spencer. Legends may be fascinating, but so are the realities from which they are derived.

Reading, Viewing and Listening

For more on Mary Spencer, see Wilf Schmidt, "Mary Spencer, Kamloops Photographer, 1899-1909" in *Kamloops—One Hundred Years of Community* (Sonotek, 1993).

The growing body of literature about Bill Miner clearly attests to his continuing popularity. See Mark Dugan and John Bossenecker: *The Grey Fox: The True Story of Bill Miner, Last of the Old-Time Bandits* (University of Oklahoma Press, 1992), *Old Bill Miner* (Heritage House, 2001), Stan Sauerwein: *Gentleman Train Robber: The Daring Exploits of Bill Miner* (Altitude, 2005). The best assessment of the character and career of Bill Miner is also the most recent: see Peter Grauer's *Interred with Their Bones: Bill Miner in Canada* (Tillicum, 2006).

Musicians and television producers continue to examine his career. Songs written to celebrate the scoundrel include 'Bill Miner' by Stu Phillips, "Bill Miner's Jailbreak" by the Kettle Valley Brakemen, and Gary Fjellgaard's "Back When Billy Robbed Trains." The National Film Board released a short animated cartoon about Bill Miner in the late 1970s, the History Channel recently featured Bill Miner on their "Manhunt" series, and the Biography Channel has announced that coming soon is a programme entitled "The Hunt for Bill Miner."

For fictional accounts of both Miner and Spencer, see *Sisters of Grass* by Theresa Kishkan (Goose Lane, 2000), and the film *The Grey Fox* (Mercury Pictures, 1982). The film's soundtrack with music by Michael Conway Baker and the Chieftains (DRG Records, 1983) is still available, as is the companion CD to the Two River Junction Musical Review.

Kamloops Collectables

When Stephen Colbert asked his television guest, US historian Doris Kearns Goodwin, why historians are so excessively interested in the past, she explained it is because historical individuals are just so damned interesting. With the same welcome absence of serious analysis, surely that explanation can be applied to historical objects. Physical items from time periods other than our own possess mysteries and significance that are just plain interesting. Often we are perplexed by an item from the past, having no understanding of what its utility may have been. More often though, we fully understand an object's use, but are fascinated by the sense it conveys of being from another time and another place.

When these objects are from ancient civilisations, they are called artifacts, are treated with respect—often with reverence—and are displayed in museums. When they are of more recent origin, we call them antiques or collectables and they attract the attention of a wide range of investors, collectors and curators. At the bottom of this hierarchy are ephemera. Churned out during the twentieth century, the little odds and ends and pieces and products that most people discarded without a second thought are often just as suggestive of the past as their more highly regarded collectable cousins.

The lines that separate collectables from ephemera—and junk from both—are indistinct and constantly shifting. (And there will be no attempt to define those lines here!) What is thought to be a treasure by one individual is commonly seen as nothing more than trash by another. Souvenirs and memories, too, are matters of individual choice and taste. While some visitors might leave a community with mass produced souvenirs or memories of a tournament, others will cherish a theatre programme, a local CD, an impression of the landscape. Memories and impressions are often the result of chance and serendipity, and objects that are evocative for one person can possess no resonance at all for another.

The following pages contain a truly random selection of items that are identified with Kamloops. Some, quite literally, are the brands and labels of products that originated here; others are objects that have some other connection to the city and its environs. To different people, some of these items will be memorable, others insignificant. The selection presented here was determined solely by what came to hand for the purposes of this little book. Of course, there are hundreds of omissions—items sought but not located, or items simply not known of—that could or should be included. However, if even a few of those presented here provide some insight into the local past or bring a smile of recognition to individual readers, they will once more have served a purpose.

Opposite: Kami the Fish was criticised for a non-fishlike appearance and a willingness to carry a gun, but he/she was arguably the most versatile symbol ever employed to promote the Kamloops area.

Courtesy of Joyce Klassen and Don Wilson

KAMI
KAMLOOPS
B.C.
KAMLOOPS
KAMI
B.C.'s TOURNAMENT
CAPITAL
KAMLOOPS
B.C.
KAMLOOPS SPOOLMAK DAYS '76
"KAMI"
1ST ANNUAL
Aug.27-Sept.6
KAMI
KAMLOOPS, B.C.
SPOOLMAK
KAMLOOPS
Kamloops
Spoolmak
Days
1980
AUGUST
20-24
"KAMI"
KAMI OVERLANDER
DAYS
1969
KAMI OVERLANDER DAYS - KAMLOOPS
1970
KAMI OVERLANDER DAYS - KAMLOOPS
KAMI SAM
1971

Above and Opposite: This colourful selection of apple box labels suggests that the Kamloops fruit-packing industry was once a major contributor to the local economy.

Collection of Larry and Lorna Kotz

CAMLOUPS
BRAND
SALES AGENTS
B.C.
B.C. TREE FRUITS LTD. KELOWNA, B.C.
CONTENTS
ONE VOLUME
BUSHEL
CANADIAN
APPLES
PACKED AND SHIPPED BY
THOMPSON VALLEY GROWERS
CO-OPERATIVE EXCHANGE
KAMLOOPS, B.C.
CANADA

"MAC-KI"
BRAND
CANADIAN APPLES
PACKED AND SHIPPED BY
MAIN LINE SHIPPERS LIMITED
KAMLOOPS, B.C.

Above and Opposite: An indication of the range of soft drinks once bottled in Kamloops.
Courtesy of Winston Putnam

HUB
CITY
BRAND
HUB
CITY
BRAND
KAMLOOPS
TRANS CANADA
TRADE MARK REGISTERED

PEPSI-COLA
A SPARKLING
BEVERAGE
PEPSI-COLA
REFRESHING · SATISFYING

Few current Kamloops residents recall the days of the Inland Cigar Company, but many will remember dining at the W.K.

Courtesy of Joyce Klassen and Don Wilson

Supported by a community fundraising effort, the Kamloops High School Band toured Europe in 1954. Recorded by the CBC, their disc was pressed in the USA.

Above and Opposite: Kamloops has always been a sports town—as pucks and patches indicate.

KAMLOOPS
CHIEFS

Kamloops
1962
MINOR
SOFTBALL
BOYS
LEAGUE

1966-67
Midgets
KAMLOOPS
CITY LEAGUE CHAMPS

Commemoratives, a token from a private club, a police button, and a Depression-era dog tag. Courtesy of Joyce Klassen and Don Wilson

Kamloops, B.C.

These were the main attractions at Riverside Park not so very long ago.

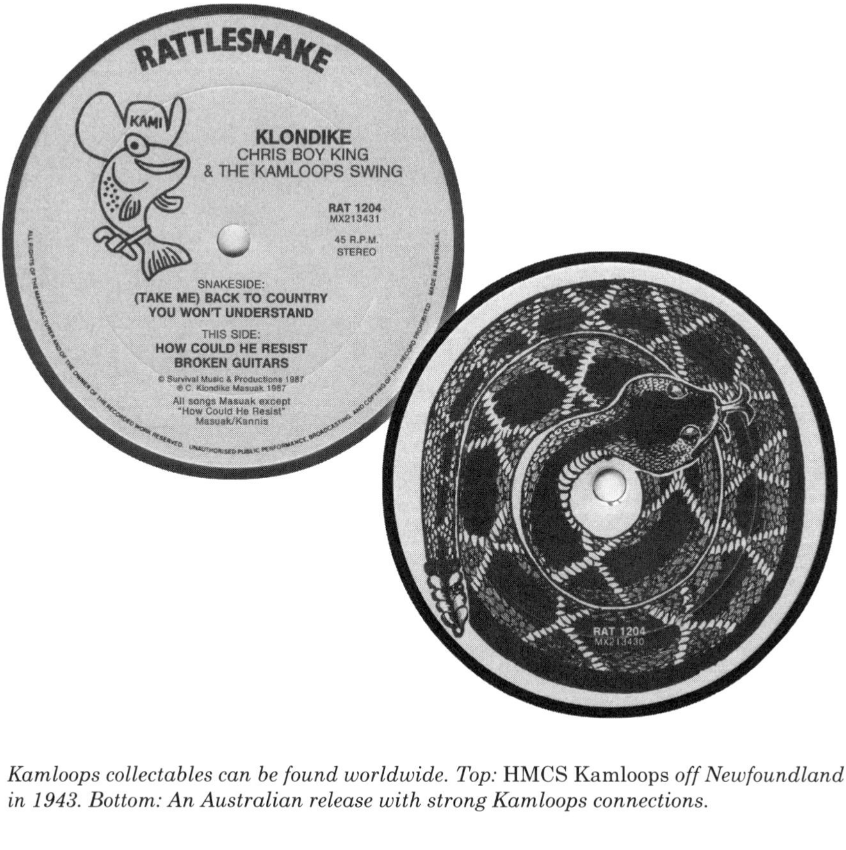

Kamloops collectables can be found worldwide. Top: HMCS Kamloops *off Newfoundland in 1943. Bottom: An Australian release with strong Kamloops connections.*

Few plates from local restaurants have survived as many decades as these two.
Courtesy of Joyce Klassen and Don Wilson

Paper ephemera—all are part of the local past.
Courtesy of Joyce Klassen and Don Wilson

An unusual view of Kamloops village found in G. Mercer Adam's Canada: From Sea to Sea, *published in 1888.*

Perhaps the rarest of all Kamloops collectables: the best known photograph of Bill Miner showing Mary Spencer's studio imprint. Courtesy of Don Stewart

Representing Kamloops: Nelson Riis and Phil Gaglardi

Politicians are rather like popular songs. We can hear them—or hear of them—almost daily for a certain period of time, but after they fall off the charts we give them little thought. New tunes and fresh voices attract our attention. This loss of interest in past politicians seems to apply equally to the civic, provincial and federal varieties and is unaffected by political party. When writing in 1950 about Kamloops politics, journalist Bruce Hutchison asked, "What Kamloopian will ever forget that three provincial party leaders and two future premiers were chosen in convention here?" The answer to that question, for many years now, has been that all of us have probably forgotten. More modern politicians fare little better. Even E. Davie Fulton and Len Marchand, both of whom enjoyed lengthy careers and significant federal portfolios, are only marginally more distinct in local memory than the dozens of lesser figures who have strutted their stuff on the local political stage over the past few decades.

Apart from current office holders, however, there remain two individuals who have not yet been relegated to the yesterday file. Both have names that are readily identifiable by residents of Kamloops—even amongst those who have moved here only recently—and each, during his heyday, became closely identified with Kamloops in the minds of people outside constituency borders. Both were seen as spokesmen for this community to a far greater extent than would normally be expected of non-civic politicians. People from Victoria to Halifax would respond to the names Phil Gaglardi and Nelson Riis with a knowledgeable: "Ah, yes—Kamloops."

Unlike certain other federal and provincial ridings, Kamloops is not an easy prize for any political party. It has been represented provincially in the past fifty years by successful Social Credit, Liberal and NDP candidates, and federally by MPs carrying the banners of the NDP, Progressive Conservatives, Liberals, Alliance and Conservatives. Federally, it has the courage to go against the grain, though provincially it tends to bend with the prevailing wind. Perhaps a mixed metaphor like that could be allowed just this once because the careers of Phil Gaglardi and Nelson Riis suggest that Kamloops, politically speaking, has indeed been an amalgam of incompatible parts.

Phil Gaglardi

Philip Gaglardi was born in Silverdale near Mission in 1913. He moved to Kamloops in 1945 when he and his wife Jennie were asked to take over as co-pastors at the small Pentecostal church here. Gaglardi accepted the invitation only after CFJC radio owner Ian Clark agreed to let him broadcast a daily radio programme. The congregation purchased and repaired the former United Church building on Seymour Street, renamed it Calvary Temple, and saw their numbers grow substantially. Gaglardi made a local name for himself through his "Chapel in the Sky" radio programme and by assisting in the fight to contain the flood waters of 1948. He resisted pressure to enter civic politics, saying his life's work lay with his church, but he could not resist the invitation to stand as a candidate in Kamloops for the new BC Social Credit Party in 1952.

He won that election handily. Social Credit then turned its minority of 1952 into a majority and governed the province of British Columbia for twenty years. For all of those years, Phil Gaglardi was the MLA for Kamloops. But he was more than just that. First as minister of public works, then as minister of highways, and finally, after a brief period of banishment from cabinet, as minister of welfare, Gaglardi was almost always at or near the centre of provincial power. For fifteen of those twenty years, he guided and supervised the modernization of British Columbia's highway and ferry systems—achievements that even his detractors could not attempt to minimize. Other provinces, too, pressed ahead with extensive improvements to their transportation systems in the two decades following the Second World War, but the geographic realities of British Columbia, in comparison, presented a far greater challenge. The impressive system of roads and ferries in place in this province by the mid 1960s, therefore, represented a greater achievement than improvements elsewhere.

Campaign pin.
Courtesy of Winston Putnam

However, even in connection with that achievement, Gaglardi gave his detractors much to focus upon. He drew the political paparazzi of his day like flies to honey because he could always be relied upon, if not for a story, at least for a quote that could be made into a story. Part of the attraction was due to his knack of mangling the meaning of words in rambling speeches to the Legislature, on the election trail, and in off-the-cuff responses to reporters' questions. BC politics has produced a wealth of quotable quotes over the years, but the most memorable single sentence may still be Gaglardi's "If I am telling a lie, it is because I think I am telling the truth." In addition, his willingness to speak his mind—regardless of political consequences—received much attention from friends and foes alike. For example, when women were pressing for social and economic equality with their male counterparts circa 1970, he asked, "If God didn't want you to be women, why didn't he make you men?" Such statements and the reaction to them kept Gaglardi constantly in the spotlight.

Critics were always at his heels due to the whiff of scandal that dogged him so persistently throughout his career. Allegations of fraud, corruption, nepotism and more, and the subsequent exonerations that never quite managed completely to clear the air are all part of the Gaglardi legacy. In this respect, Gaglardi was his own worst enemy. He seemed unable to comprehend the requirement of political transparency. If due process threatened to slow him down, he would ignore it (that is, if he had even enquired about due process). In modern parlance, the optics surrounding Gaglardi's methods were poor. Extremely rocky relations with provincial civil servants and doubts about his personal integrity were the inevitable result.

Because of differing perceptions, people's attitudes to Gaglardi more often than not boiled down to what was actually Gaglardi's stock in trade as a minister of religion—a matter of faith. People either had faith in him or they lacked faith in him. This separation was at the heart of the "Gaglardi divide"—a sharp difference of opinion that left few remaining on the middle ground of indifference. The division was in evidence both outside Social Credit and within it. Gaglardi had a knack of impressing people, and the party sought to exploit that knack during election campaigns by sending him throughout the province in attempts to sway voter preferences. These forays were not consistently successful—some voters made up their minds to support other parties immediately after hearing Gaglardi speak; others just as immediately turned to Social Credit. As a morale booster for the local party faithful, however, Gaglardi's visits were an unqualified success. He could always count on ovations from bedrock Social Credit.

Within the party leadership, however, were many who became increasingly uncomfortable with Gaglardi's controversial style and pronouncements. Though the defeat of the Social Credit government in 1972 is attributable to many factors, amongst them was the widespread perception that Gaglardi sought to succeed

Phil Gaglardi. The steady gaze and pinstriped suit convey an image of power in this official portait. Kamloops Museum and Archives photograph number 5755

W.A.C. Bennett as premier. Though he never lost the approval of the party rank and file, it is ironic that Social Credit itself was divided over the prospect of Gaglardi as leader.

Gaglardi's popularity confounded pundits at the time and it confounds them still. He defeated far more credible politicians along the way (E. Davie Fulton most notably) and survived scandals that would have hobbled most politicians. In the early 1950s, he belonged to the rebel party in BC politics, but as that party sought and achieved respectability, absorbing much of the old provincial establishment in the process, Gaglardi never lost his individual rebel image. In fact, it grew over the years to the point that it is now the foundation for the place of honour he occupies in Kamloops political history. From various local perspectives, he was the one who stood up against attacks from jealous provincial bureaucrats, or from the nitpicking coastal media, or the tweedy old guard Liberal-Conservatives, or the socialist hordes, and finally even the attacks from misguided elements within his own party. Somehow he morphed almost into the guise of an "outlaw" politician.

Gaglardi was finally defeated as the NDP swept to power in 1972. The defeat was not so much due to the fact that the voters of Kamloops had turned against him; they had simply turned elsewhere. He concentrated on family business ventures for so many years that few anticipated a return to the political arena. However, in 1988, he was persuaded out of political retirement to run for mayor of Kamloops—a development that was seen either as a welcome return or an unfortunate resurrection, de-

BC premier W.A.C. Bennett with Phil Gaglardi in Kamloops.
Kamloops Museum and Archives photograph number 5751

pending on from which side of the Gaglardi divide it was viewed. Though, as promised, he brought much attention to the city of Kamloops, his term as mayor is not generally considered a success. His image as yesterday's politician was at odds with the city's emerging wish to be seen as a modern community, and his inability to cope with bureaucratic necessities resulted in the same strained relations with municipal employees and politicians as it had with their provincial counterparts during his tenure as a cabinet minister. His status as something of a legend protected him to some extent from criticism, but his decision not to seek a second term was generally not regretted.

Over the years, Gaglardi was known to complain that there was nothing named after him despite his achievements as highways minister. The complaint ignored the fact of the road that connects Simon Fraser University with the Lougheed Highway in Burnaby. Named after Gaglardi in 1970 despite student objections, the connector quickly established and retains a reputation as something of a speedway. The former highways minister would have felt right at home on Gaglardi Way. He should also feel at home with the statue placed in the square that now bears his name at the corner of Seymour Street and Second Avenue in Kamloops. The decision to place a statue there followed the unsuccessful attempt in 2005 to rename Overlander Bridge in Gaglardi's honour—a proposal that resulted in such widespread protest that it was quickly withdrawn.

Both the erection of the statue and the controversy surrounding the attempt to change the name of the bridge have renewed the local debate on the merits of Kamloops' most famous politician. That the debate remains so lively is an indication of the impact he had on this community. To some extent, the statue can be seen as a testament to the political independence the voters of the city once exercised in returning to office time and time again an individual whose faults they knew all too well, but who they felt deserved their trust. Few Canadian politicians can expect to achieve legendary status. But Gaglardi seems on the verge of doing so, even if it is as a flawed anti-establishment figure. (Much like that other outlaw so beloved by Kamloops—must be something in the air down there around Silverdale.) And if he does obtain that status, ironically, it will not have been through achievement alone, but rather through a combination of achievement and controversy. In other words, both sides of the Gaglardi divide—detractors and supporters—have created the legend of Flying Phil.

He has already been the subject of a stage play. Can song and cinema be too far behind?

Nelson Riis

Ironically, a man who never held a government portfolio comes closest to giving Gaglardi a run for his money as the city's best remembered local politician. He has the advantage of having been in office fairly recently, and it is most unlikely that he harbours any illusions of becoming a local legend or of seeing a statue raised in his honour. Nevertheless, the career of Nelson Riis provides both interesting parallels and contrasts with that of Phil Gaglardi.

Like Gaglardi, Riis is not a native son of Kamloops. Born in High River, Alberta in 1942, he taught at John Tod Elementary School and Kamloops Secondary School in the 1960s before finishing a Masters degree at UBC and accepting a position in the geography department at the fledgling Cariboo College. Unlike Gaglardi, he was not at all coy about expressing an interest in a career in politics. He was elected as an alderman of Kamloops City Council in 1973 and remained on council for five years before switching to School Board in 1978. By that time, his grander political ambitions were well known. People wondered only when he would seek to achieve those ambitions, which party would attract him, and whether provincial or federal politics would be his chosen battleground.

All questions were answered in 1980 when Joe Clark's short-lived minority Conservative government self-destructed in Ottawa. Riis sought and won the nomination of a party that had never finished better than a distant third in the federal riding of

Nelson Riis. The long hair was gone by the late 1980s, but the John Denver good looks remained. Courtesy of Shirley Rhodes

Kamloops-Shuswap, a huge constituency that stretched from Salmon Arm to Savona to Blue River. After an exciting campaign, the residents of Kamloops-Shuswap, for the first time, found themselves represented in Ottawa by an MP from the New Democratic Party of Canada. The riding had gone against the tide, ignoring both the nationally resurgent Liberals and the traditional strength of the Conservatives in the BC interior. Many local residents simply could not believe it: Nelson Riis—Kamloops—NDP MP.

NDP leader Ed Broadbent with Kamloops MP Nelson Riis.

Courtesy of Shirley Rhodes

The result was widely viewed as an anomaly. Political opponents believed (and political supporters feared) it would not be repeated. They were all wrong. Riis went on to enjoy four more electoral victories, serving for twenty-one years as the MP for a riding that went through two name changes and boundary alterations, but which always contained Kamloops at its centre.

He rose quickly within his party, taking on various parliamentary responsibilities, becoming NDP House Leader for a decade, and holding the positions of caucus chair and Finance Critic. He managed to survive the massive Conservative surge in the 1984 election and the Reform Party sweep of western Canada in 1993, following which he was one of the few New Democrats left standing.

Throughout the 1980s, Riis had the advantage of belonging to the party led by the popular Ed Broadbent, but his repeated electoral successes were due primarily to his own qualities and efforts. He devoted a great deal of time to constituency work and held regular and innovative "town hall" meetings within the city and in the outlying communities. Though he consistently expressed support for his party's positions, he worked hard to be seen as a moderate within the NDP. So successful was this positioning that rumours frequently circulated in Kamloops that Riis was on the verge of crossing the floor to the governing party of the day in Ottawa—either to the Liberals or perhaps even to Mulroney's Conservatives.

Riis also benefited from a benign relationship with the local media. Photogenic and articulate, he was an acknowledged master at creating media interest in his proposals and pronouncements, regardless of their significance or substance. For nearly a quarter of a century, few editions of local newspapers appeared without a mention of Nelson Riis somewhere in their pages. And while Gaglardi benefited from radio exposure, Riis found a ready platform on both CFJC television and community television programming. Provincial and national media, too, seemed to beat a path to his door whenever an opinion was required on his party's position on issues of the day. He became one of the most recognisable political faces and voices in the country through radio and print interviews and television appearances. (Though perhaps not necessarily a good thing, he remains the only Kamloops politician to have attracted the attention of the Royal Canadian Air Farce.)

There certainly was a "Riis divide" during his twenty-year incumbency. Despite his apparent popularity between elections, he never achieved more than 40% of the vote on election days, as traditional Liberal and Conservative party allegiances remained strong within the riding. Critics were frustrated by his continued electoral success, describing him as something of a Teflon man, often asking what he really stood for and questioning what benefits he brought to Kamloops and environs. To this latter question, he could offer no uncontested response. Whatever he pointed to as resulting from his efforts, supporters of the governing Liberals or Conservatives could just as readily claim as a benefit deriving from government priorities—and not from lobbying by the local Opposition MP.

His reputation as the consummate politician received a self-inflicted setback during the election campaign of 1997 when he promised that his re-election would result in the creation of 10,000 local jobs. For those with long memories, it sounded like vintage Gaglardi hyperbole. Voters overlooked it and re-elected him nevertheless. However, the subsequent three years brought recurring indications that the power of his political touch was weakening. He sustained his steady presence in the local media, but the themes and topics often appeared almost too familiar. The federal NDP, under leaders less popular after Broadbent's retirement, was undergoing a prolonged debate about political direction. In the process, Riis supported a move to a more centrist philosophy, clashing particularly with New West-

This campaign slogan from 1997 indicates that Gaglardi was not alone in his ability to mangle the language.

Courtesy of Sheila Park

minster's Svend Robinson both personally and politically. Many within the party questioned the wisdom and motivation of his decision to write for the right-wing Fraser Institute.

Riis may have been simply acknowledging that the political winds were changing. If so, the attempt to change with them proved unsuccessful. In the election of 2000, Riis finished a distant second to Reform candidate Betty Hinton. The endorsement of popular Kamloops mayor Mel Rothenburger could not counter a combination of the profound unpopularity of the provincial New Democrats, the surge of support the leadership of Stockwell Day brought to the Reform Party in western Canada, and the widely acknowledged factor of Riis fatigue in the electorate. Yet, like Gaglardi's defeat in 1972, Riis's was not fundamentally a personal loss. It was the result of an electorate seeking a new voice, alternative options, a change that was perhaps overdue. For nearly 50 percent of the voters in this constituency, the Reform Party fit the bill precisely in that election.

The lingering affection felt for Nelson Riis is not based on support for the particular part of the political spectrum he championed; it is based on an appreciation for the manner in which he represented us to the world outside our constituency borders. He provided a distinct counterweight to the prevalent perception—the strength of which was yet another testament to the durability of Gaglardi's legacy—that Kamloops produced only blowhard politicians of narrow understanding. If his full legacy remains indistinct, that much at least is clear. Perhaps the final assessment of the place of Nelson Riis in local history will be completed only by the ultimate results of the financial scheme that many local residents invested in at his suggestion. No longer a resident of Kamloops, Riis expresses little interest in returning to politics either here or elsewhere.

Conclusion: Nelson and Phil

There are many parallels between the careers of Phil Gaglardi and Nelson Riis. Neither man was born in Kamloops, yet each came to be seen as the definitive voice of Kamloops politics. Each enjoyed and exploited the media spotlight. Each polled particularly well on the north shore, thrived on public attention (and had a knack for creating it), and represented their constituents for twenty years before surprising yet predictable defeats. On the other hand, the differences between the two are clear. Their political philosophies contrasted as sharply as did their personal styles. Gaglardi occupied a seat on the government benches in Victoria and was almost always in Cabinet; Riis sat on the Opposition side in the House of Commons in Ottawa. Although Riis belonged to the party generally perceived to have been the most anti-establishment in Canadian politics, it is Gaglardi who was much the greater rebel.

Civic resurrection aside, Gaglardi's prominence in the 1950s and 1960s was sufficiently long ago that, like everything else from those decades, it can now be made into the stuff of myth and legend and history. The political career of Nelson Riis is far too recent for any of that. Moreover, his consensus style of politics and the general lack of any sustained controversy surrounding him provide little of the grist required by the mills of myth and legend. If the question becomes one of which man is likely to remain longer in local memory, the answer is clear. Unless Riis surprises everyone with a return to local politics, Gaglardi's the one.

Reading and Listening

Phil Gaglardi is the only Kamloops politician ever to have attracted a biographer. See Mel Rothenburger: *Friend o' Mine* (Victoria, BC: Orca, 1991). The author of the article appearing here owes much to that biography. Considerations of Gaglardi, of his achievements and the controversies that surrounded him appear throughout the extensive literature describing British Columbia's twenty years of Social Credit government. Few people recall that Gaglardi recorded four religious songs in Vancouver in the early 1950s and had them privately released on Arrex records.

Nelson Riis has yet to receive biographical attention. A general Google search of the Internet calls up a potpourri of articles that date from the latter stages of his political life. His entire career is a matter of public record that can be followed in the pages of the local and national newspapers of the day and in publications assessing the NDP in federal politics. Riis is known to have dabbled in painting, but, as far as the current author is aware, never made a record.

That's all, folks!